Chrysanthemum Culture

Dedicated

to

Sri Subrata Goswami

an ardent chrysanthemum grower of the young generation, who succeeds in growing mums to perfection

Chrysanthemum Culture

S.C. DEY

ABHINAV PUBLICATIONS

abhinav publications
New Delhi

First published in India 2002

Publishers
Shakti Malik
ABHINAV PUBLICATIONS
E-37, Hauz Khas,
New Delhi - 110 016 (INDIA)
Phones: 6566387, 6562784, 6524658
Fax: 91-11-6857009
e-mail: shakti@nde.vsnl.net.in
Website: http//www.abhinavexports.com

ISBN 81-7017-413-9

Lasertypeset in 11/13.2 Garamond by
S.R. Enterprises
Lajpat Nagar-IV
New Delhi-110024
Phone: 011-6236663

Printed at
D.K. Fine Art Press Pvt. Ltd.
Ashok Vihar, Delhi

Contents

Appendices

Preface

Whether taken up as a hobby or profession flower growing or floriculture specially the culture of chrysanthemum provides an endless field for pleasure and study.

The primary purpose of this book is to help the amateur chrysanthemum growers understand the principles and procedures for raising blooms of an improved quality. Professionally advanced people such as nurserymen, park and garden personnel, commercial flower growers and the progressive growers also find it useful particularly for making optimum flower production for garden display, show benches or cut-flower markets. The students of the horticultural faculty will have the major portion of its texts written in details analysing the horticultural principles based on the latest developments in this field.

Since from remote past chrysanthemum has been a favourite of serious flower growers there must be some important reasons for its thus being placed in the forefront of all other flowering perennials treated as an annual. In the first place no other seasonal flower has the lasting quality of chrysanthemums. No other cultivated annual can be compared with chrysanthemum in regard to the delicacy of beauties. The range of colours is so wide, the variety of forms is so great and the multitude of novelties is rushing so fast that a sensible grower can well satisfy his thirst for beauty, longing for variation and craze for the new.

There are many volumes on this subject written mostly by the authors of the transatlantic regions, which furnish their experiences about the cultural methods of their cold climates. They are being imported and sold in large numbers in this country. But we can utilize very little of their data in our hot climate with our indigenous resources.

Utmost care has been taken to express the things as lucidly as possible facing the difficulties of writing a technical literature in the popular style.

I am very thankful to Messrs H. Woolman Ltd. Birmingham, for their kind permission to reproduce the history of Chrysanthemum in this work. It would be admitted on all hands that any book of its kind can never be complete without such a long glorious history of the flower.

I express my gratitude here to those who have extended their help in preparing the manuscript and supplying the photographs for illustration.

15 March, 1999 S.C. Dey

Introduction

To become a successful grower of chrysanthemum one must treat one's plants as a mother tends her child, giving them care and attention they deserve for producing blooms to perfection. A Chinese proverb says: "The best manure is grower's footprints." In other words your plants need intimate care. It is not an exaggerated fact that I have learnt from my experience, if we treat our mums as the members of our family there will not be any failure and disappointment; just as a child with proper care and attention attains healthy maturity, so with our chrysanthemums. With due consideration, that is, doing the right things in proper time, not neglecting the cultural details quality blooms can be obtained. The more one will translate this into action the better will be the result.

The beginners should start with the medium-flowered varieties, because they will find them more accommodating than the large-flowered cultivars. The pompons are very easy to grow. The plant with numerous bunches of flowers forms a massive head which is worth displaying. The new entrants can succeed in growing such plants with less difficulties.

It is, however, a good policy to form the nucleus of your selection by the tried and proved varieties on which one can rely with confidence.

India has a great variety of climates ranging from a frosty hill station to a scorching desert. The variety of soils and climate calls for a variety of treatments in the cultural operations. As it is not possible to deal with the problems of every region owing to climatic differences the whole has been classified into two on the basis of the degree of rainfall. As the heavy rainfall is a deterrent agent to chrysanthemum culture the growers should take precaution against it as laid down in the chapter entitled 'Protection from Rains'.

The popular phrase "Learn by mistakes" has its significance, that can also be applied to chrysanthemum culture, but to a very limited extent. In the sphere of chrysanthemum culture the new growers must have instructions from the experienced growers or they will run the risk of failure leading to frustrations.

Most people think that chrysanthemum is a delicate plant that needs very careful handling. But this is not the fact. Because in the rains it needs protection from showers but in all other seasons it thrives well like other garden herbs. During monsoon the soil fungus attacks the growing roots that cannot function normally resulting in wilting of the plants. Those growers who are unable to protect the plants from the rains by putting them under the transparent sheds should start growing from October. The monsoon from the most part of the mainland recedes in the first week of October. From the beginning of September the intensity of deluge decreases, i.e. the showers become less frequent. Therefore one can start planting from the second week of September.

Fred W. Loads writes in his book Chrysanthemum for Everyone that growing of chrysanthemum is not more difficult than that of marigold. I too am of the same view and have tried to prove it through the simple technique discussed in the text of this book. The principle in view is to simplify the complex cultural practices which are in vogue. And this is the reason why the new growers can hardly follow those practices to be successful early.

Like us chrysanthemums also have their identity. In other words, they have varietal identity with individual likings that demand separate treatments. So the growers should be careful to learn the differences in their requirements.

In the developed countries the newly introduced cultivars are put to trial in the trial gardens to assess their merits in that soil and climate. The chrysanthemum societies of the respective regions publish the trial ground reports in their bulletins that enlighten the growers as to the characteristics of the varieties concerned. On account of this the growers knowing the details of the varieties introduced succeed in raising standard blooms even in the first attempt. The nurserymen append the tips obtained from the trial ground to their trade catalogues. How the imported varieties will perform here in our climates should be ascertained by trials, which is essentially needed to grow them successfully in the first attempt. The new growers should refrain from growing the delicate varieties. Because they need more details which must be followed in their culture. On the contrary the hardy varieties respond well to the general cultural methods.

To improve the quality of the blooms the soil round the plant should be rammed to make it hard. Because the plants grown in the loose soil cannot produce compact blooms. The new growers may avoid this operation. But the exhibitor aiming at winning prizes must not neglect the operation of ramming.

The propagation by shoot cuttings is very easy. They root through all the seasons. The new growers may fail to get their cuttings rooted satisfactorily. They hardly find out the reason. Apparently all the requirements are satisfied, still the failure. In this case they are advised to make the mother plants disease-free by spraying fungicides regularly. Secondly, the mother plants that supply cuttings should not get drenched frequently in showers. Thirdly, they should enjoy direct sunlight in the most part of the day. In the relevant chapter the details have been discussed.

Some believe that the use of selected fertilizers only can ensure good blooms. This is not the fact, which can be explained thus: Chrysanthemum, like all other plants, needs nitrogen in plenty. Oilcake, urea, bloodmeal, hoof and hornmeal, fishmeal etc. are rich in nitrogen. By using any of these ingredients or a combination of any two or more chrysanthemum can be grown successfully. But the use of the ingredients is different.

Originating new cultivars is scarcely attempted here. To attract the new growers the breeding techniques have been simplified. To detect the spontaneous mutants and perpetuation thereof for their varietal identity are of great importance. All these have been discussed lucidly. To reinforce the text the book has been illustrated profusely with figures as well as photographs. Some odds are incorporated in the appendices, though they are last but not the least.

1
History of Chrysanthemum

It was in 926 A.D. that the Micado Uda of Japan, an ardent lover of the flower, set the fashion by issuing an edict commanding that the whole realm be scanned, every garden ransacked, and the choicest specimens assembled at his palace in Tokyo, for the delectation of himself and his courtiers.

An ancient lineage

That was a thousand years ago, but the queen of oriental flowers has a lineage twice as ancient. It is a far cry from the yellow, wrinkled Mongol in his garden in far-off Cathay two millenniums ago, by the patient toil of a lifetime evolving the first cultivated varieties from the little wayside weed, to the city clerk in his superb lovingly tending his plants that they may bear the magnificent, elaborate blooms of today, as diverse as fantastically contorted dancers with streaming wind-blown hair, and glowing anemones waving their sensative tentacles and perfect spheres of subtly delicate shades.

For ages the Chinese have esteemed the "liki", as they call it, only less than a peony. Celebrated statesmen and soldiers, famed philosophers and poets were honoured also that they produced, by devoted care, new and splendid varieties.

A poet and an epicure, a connoisseur of all refined and subtle pleasures, was T'ao Ming-yang, who walked in his garden more than fifteen hundred years ago, amid the myriad dainty or superb, graceful or quaint chrysanthemums that his skill had brought to birth. He was the greatest of all Chinese breeders. When he died the city where he deigned to dwell changed its name to Chuhsein, the city of Chrysanthemums.

A royal symbol in Japan

At a period far back, near the beginning of even Chinese annals, the chrysanthemum migrated to Japan, and there became invested with almost sacred attributes. It became the symbol of the sacred ruling dynasty, and as the sign, the crest as it were, of the Micado, its use is strictly forbidden in any design save for Imperial purposes. It is reproduced in conventionalised form on State documents of high importance, emblazoned upon the doors of Imperial carriages, engraved or enamelled or set with jewels on the hilts and scabbards of the swords of the most exalted servants of the Emperor. The highest honour he can bestow is the order of the Chrysanthemum, created for and scrupulously confined to Royal and noble personages.

When and whence the first foreign varieties came to Europe is not known, but it seems at any rate very probable that the Dutch, those enthusiastic and skilful horticulturists, introduced them when they enjoyed so great a share of commerce with the East. The first entry of foreign varieties into this country that can be traced occurred in 1764, from Japan. What became of them is not recorded. Then just a quarter of a century later, no fewer than 1,000 varieties were brought back to France by Captain Blanchard, whose vessel plied between Marseilles and the Orient. Only one out of them survived, and was propagated, the Old Purple, as it was called much later. For another quarter of a century this appears to have remained the only kind to be found in Western gardens. Today Old Purple has many descendants, and some of the prize-winning blossoms at the annual show may very likely be ultimately derived from it.

One hundred years ago

There were 27 kinds growing in the Horticultural Gardens at

Chiswick in 1824. The following year John Damper Park, who had been despatched to China as a collector by the Royal Horticultural Society, arrived with 700 new varieties. It became the most talked-of flower in the land, and all gardeners who prided themselves on being up-to-date were prating of "mums".

In two years a fair-sized exhibition was very successful. The reign of the queen flower of Autumn had commenced. Thenceforward its history in the West becomes so complex, as multitudinous kinds were produced, that one can mention only the salient events.

Chinese and Japanese varieties

But long ago the huge double type, with petals all incurved, forming an absolutely regular formal sphere of one colour, were very highly esteemed. Then, in 1882, upon the termination of the Chinese War, Robust Fortune, a notable Scottish botanist and traveller, was despatched by the Royal Horticultural Society to collect plants in China, and among the beautiful flowers his travels were the means of introducing into Europe, were new varieties of chrysanthemums, particularly the small flowered pompons, the tiny pink and white blooms which had originated from the Chusan daisy.

In 1862 Fortune introduced the grotesque-flowered Japanese sorts, popular for decorative purposes. The Japanese varieties provide a wide range of colour and form, of habit and times of flowering.

One would suppose, from general observation, that our taste is moving closer to the ideas of the Japanese, unrivalled in producing marvellous symmetrical masses of blossoms. Not always is the aim to produce a few gigantic flowers on long, thin, almost leafless stems, but more often to have bushy plants with plenty of foliage and great number of short-stemmed medium-sized blooms.

From "Birmingham Mail"
Anthony Clyne

2

Botanical Features

The chrysanthemum, literally means the Gold Flower, is a genus of *Compositae*. The plants are shrubs or herbaceous and develop suckers like peppermint (*Mentha*), Mint etc. Suckers are also branches originated from the subterranean part of the stem of the parent plant. The suckers run horizontally under the surface of the soil for a little distance before they come out into view. They develop adventitious roots from the nodes of their underground parts.

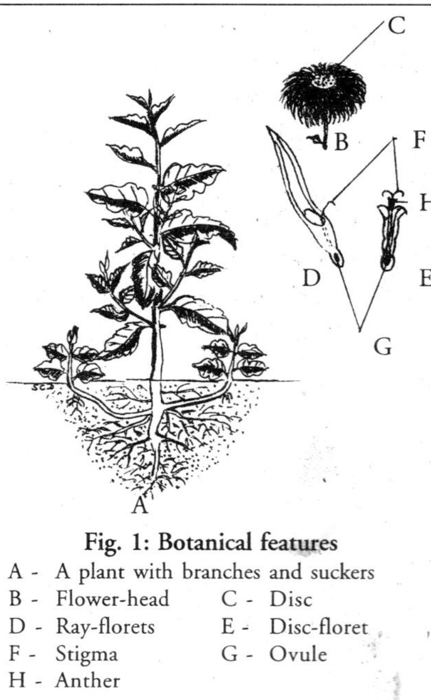

Fig. 1: Botanical features

A - A plant with branches and suckers
B - Flower-head C - Disc
D - Ray-florets E - Disc-floret
F - Stigma G - Ovule
H - Anther

The stem of the chrysanthemum is woody and undergoes secondary growth in thickness. The leaf is simple alternate pinnatifid, that is, the incisions of the lamina or leaf blade extend less than halfway downwards the midrib. Chrysanthemums, like Dahlia, are perennial, though they are treated as

3E. A spider variety (CV. 'ACHIEVEMENT').

3C. Healthy mother plants that supply shoot cuttings. (Photo: Author)

3A. Cuttings in thumb pots for sale in Horticultural Arena (top).

3B. Cuttings in thumb pots (bottom). (Photo: Author)

3D. Myriad of pompons.

36. One-stem standards of reflexing varieties.

↑

;. Chrysanthemum is
opagated under a poly-shed in
orticultural Arena (Author's Nursery).

:. SEN RIN TSUKURI of a white spider.

101. 'ELIZABETH SHOESMITH' (Reflexed). Courtesy: Subrata Goswami

On the next page

102. A large white incurved (top).

103. 'DORRIDGE QUEEN' (Incurved). Courtesy: Subrata Goswami (bottom).

106. A large incurving of attractive colour.

104. 'AUTUMN BLAZE' (Reflexed) (top).

108. 'GENERAL PETTAIN' (Incurving) (bottom).

105. 'HEAVENLY TOUCH' (Incurved).

109. Spiders:
CV. 'YELLOW KNIGHT' (left).
CV. 'TOKYO WHITE' (right).

107. 'PETER MAY' (Reflexed).

110. 'CASA GRANDE' (Incurved). Courtesy: Subrata Goswami

111. 'SEATONS SULPHUR' (Quilled).

114. A good reflex of wide florets.

112. 'LEVIATHAN' (Incurving).

113. 'MRS DOUGLAS FOXBILL'.

121. A yellow spider.

115. 'DUKE OF KENT' (Incurved).

118. 'GARDEN STATE' (Incurved)

120. 'ROYAL PURPLE' (Spider). (Photo: Author)

122. 'TOKYO WHITE'.

123. 'YELLOW KNIGHT' (Spider).

annuals. The chrysanthemum flowers during the cold months of the year.

What is generally known to us as a flower is really an aggregation of a number of florets (small flowers) developed on a single flower-head. The florets are of two kinds — those with broad petals at the periphery are called ray-florets and those at the centre are called disc-florets which are tubular in form. These are the characteristics of the family *Compositae*. The plant is propagated by suckers, seeds or cuttings.

3

Classification

The elaborate classification of chrysanthemum often confuses the new growers. The classification is based on the shape and size of the florets, their arrangement on the head and the size of the bloom. The trade catalogues of the nurserymen of this country hardly furnish the classification. So one has to face inconvenience to select the varieties. The classification laid down in the Bulletin of the National Chrysanthemum Society (England) is highly appreciated in the chrysanthemum growing countries. The large-flowered varieties which were known as Japanese chrysanthemums until the sixties of the past century are now known as exhibition varieties.

Large-flowered varieties

INCURVED: The florets near the periphery are curved inward. Neatly arranged. The flower form is spherical. The centre of the bloom is always covered with petals. The incurved is of two types:

i) Regular incurved — when the bloom is perfectly spherical with perfect symmetry, e.g. SNOWBALL.

ii) Irregular incurved — the outer florets are

partly twisted and not so curved as in the regular incurved, e.g. ANGLE BELLE.

INCURVING: It is also known as INTERMEDIATE. Because of the formation lying between the 'Incurved' and 'Reflexed'. The florets are loosely arranged, i.e. not so compact as in the incurved, e.g. ALFRED SIMPSON.

REFLEXED: The florets are curved outwards, i.e. just the opposite of the 'Incurved', e.g. 'VALIANT'. This group is sub-divided into three distinct types:

i) Regular Reflexed — AUTUMN BLAZE.

ii) Irregular Reflexed — CORONATION PINK.

iii) Aster Reflexed — it looks like Asters, e.g. ROYAL PRINCE.

ANEMONE: The formation is peculiar. The disc is large with high disc-florets. The tip of the ray-florets is quill-shaped. It is a nice novelty.

i) Single Anemone — the rows of the ray-florets never exceed five. A plant with plenty of single anemone blooms is very charming, e.g. VINICIAN GLASS.

ii) Double Anemone — the disc is small.

SPIDER: The florets are thread-like and long, e.g. ACHIEVEMENT, FILTRATION, PUSPAHAR etc.

SEMI-DOUBLE: The ray-florets are in more than five rows. The disc is conspicuous, e.g. BRODECAR.

TUBULAR: The ray-florets are cylindrical and tubular, e.g. VALIANT.

SPOON: The tips of the ray-florets are spoon-like, e.g. CHRISTMAS TIDE.

Small-flowered varieties

ANEMONE: The shape is the same as the large type but small in size, e.g. WHITE CUSHION.

BUTTON: Very small, not bigger than a large button. The heads are compact with florets. The plants are very dwarf and hardy and produce flowers for a long time, e.g. YELLOW GEM.

KOREAN: The ray-florets are strap-like. The single Korean is that which has not more than five rows of ray-florets.

DECORATIVE: The ray-florets are like those of Korean. But the disc is not visible, e.g. WHITE DECORATIVE.

POMPON: The ray-florets are broad and nicely arranged. The shape of the bloom is spherical or hemispherical. The number of blooms is extremely great, e.g. BALRAJ SHAHNI, APSARA

CHARM OR CINERARIA: It looks like Korean type. But the diameter of a bloom does not exceed 3 cm.

A list of select varieties as well as the list of varieties published by the Chrysanthemum Society of India in 1986 have been appended at the end.

4
Soil

To produce a good bloom one must be sure about the desirable texture of the soil to be used for chrysanthemum. Before using the recommended potting compost one should thoroughly understand why the preference is given to a special type of soil texture for chrysanthemum. In other words, a grower should know the actual need of his subjects as to developing a good root system in a soil medium.

Basically there are three types of soil — clay, loam and sandy soil. Sandy soil contains less than 20 per cent of clay. It cannot hold food ingredients which when soluble are leached out along with the percolating water. Clay soil becomes very sticky after a shower. Because it absorbs and holds too much of water. Loam consists of about sixty per cent sand and fifty per cent clay. The grower having no experience cannot ascertain which type of soil is useful for the chrysanthemum culture. They generally tend to use sandy soil as they think that extremely light soil is indispensable for this purpose. They seldom know that moderately heavy loam is best for chrysanthemums. To the loam add humus at the rate of 4:1, i.e. one part of humus to four parts of loam. Humus is a decomposed vegetative matter which when mixed with a heavy soil in a right proportion improves the structure of the soil. The improved structure facilitates soil aeration. A heavy soil is compact, the pores within the soil mass are very minute. When humus is mixed thoroughly the volume and number of pores increase. In other words, the soil becomes friable and granular, the condition of a good structure. Leafmould is the best form of humus. The dung of animals that feed on grass and leaves, on decomposition can be a substitute of leafmould. Cowmanure, stable manure etc. are such materials. The potting compost for chrysanthemum should not contain cattle manure as it holds water copiously. It should be borne in mind that chrysanthemum cannot stand the stagnant moisture. In the dry months it can be controlled by judicious watering. On the contrary when the downpour is frequent the plant put under the transparent shed during the rainy months does not face this situation. Secondly, if the potting compost is rammed while potting water cannot be stagnant in the soil mass. It percolates slowly through the rammed soil which is tight.

5

Soil Reaction

It is to be remembered that chrysanthemum is a lime-loving plant. In other words, chrysanthemums do not thrive well in an acid soil. Lime is an alkali that neutralizes an acid.

Acidity and Alkalinity

There is always a certain concentration of hydrogen ions (H^+) and of hydroxyl ions (OH^-) in any aqueous solution. Their concentrations always vary. The hydrogen ions (H^+) are responsible for the acidity of the solution and hydroxyl ions (OH^-) for its alkalinity. Ionization of water takes place forming hydrogen and hydroxyl ions according to the following equation:

$$H_2O \rightleftarrows H^+ + OH^-$$

Thus any solution containing water as solvent must contain hydrogen and hydroxyl ions in its water molecules.

How Acidity and Alkalinity is measured

The chemists have already invented a scale called the P^H scale which ranges from 1-14 by which the degree of acidity or alkalinity is measured.

In this scale P^H 7 is taken as the mid-point. Any solution having P^H 7 is neutral, i.e. the solution is neither acidic nor alkaline.

In order to determine the soil reaction one should use soil testing kits. The P^H indicator paper of British Drug House (Mumbai) or E. Merk (Germany) is quite suitable to determine the hydrogen ion concentrations of an aqueous solution. The water to be used for watering the plants should be of known concentration. If neutral water is wanting the soil under cultivation should be tested at a short interval. Brackish water which is alkaline in reaction is however suitable for watering chrysanthemum. A cultural medium of P^H 7.5 is ideal for the chrysanthemum culture.

6

Soil Reaction and Nutrient Availability

The plant growth mainly depends upon the availability of nutrients, which has a definite relation to soil reaction. In other words, sufficient plant food present in the soil may not be available to plants due to soil reaction. In such cases it is useless to apply more manure to accelerate the growth of a plant.

In an acid soil plants get less nitrates and phosphates, calcium and magnesium salts. Potassium salts become unavailable in soils greater than P^H 8. This clearly explains why one must ascertain the P^H value for one's mums. The relative acidity of a soil is disturbed by unscientific manuring.

7
Manures and Fertilizers

Many substances, both organic and inorganic, are used as manures and fertilizers to feed chrysanthemums.

Manures

All organic matters, dead or excreted, when decomposed can supply plant nutrients. Hence organic matters must undergo decomposition before they can be used as a manure. Leaves, barks, twigs, fruit peels, seeds, straws and grasses become manure on decomposition. But hoof, horn, leather and bone, if pulverized, can be applied to the soil. Similarly dry fish can be a good manure. Oil seeds, after oil extraction, form a cake which is regarded as a manure. But like other vegetative matters it must decompose to be a manure. Bloodmeal is a good nitrogenous manure which boosts the vegetative growth and flower size of chrysanthemums.

Fertilizers

Many chemical substances contain plant nutrients. Certain compounds are however commercially manufactured in bulk for use as fertilizers. Such products are urea, superphosphate, muriate of potash, calcium ammonium nitrate (CAN), potassium sulphate, etc. In this country the use of chemical fertilizers has increased. Many gardeners are still not in favour of using chemical substances for feeding their plants. But a remarkable result is obtained in growth and production when fertilizers are used with plenty of organic manures. The following chemical compounds are used as fertilizers.

Urea: It is a concentrated nitrogenous fertilizer that contains 45 per cent of nitrogen. Urea contains only nitrogen and nothing else. It can be used during the soil preparation as well as top dressing or liquid manure for growing chrysanthemums. For mums it is recommended when the plants become stunted.

Ammonium sulphate: Plants obtain 21 per cent of nitrogen from this fertilizer. It also supplies sulphur. Before the introduction of urea this fertilizer was the main source of nitrogen for plants in a chemical form. Now its use is very limited. But it is highly recommended for alkaline soils, because the alkalinity is reduced by its acid reaction. Like all other nitrogenous fertilizers the use of ammonium sulphate will make chrysanthemums tall, and it will increase acidity or reduce alkalinity of a soil

Ammonium nitrate: It contains 35 per cent of nitrogen. But half of its amount is available in the nitrate form and the other half in the ammonium form. No other fertilizer except urea contains so much of nitrogen.

Di-ammonium phosphate: It contains 18 per cent of nitrogen and 48 per cent of phosphate. Its abbreviated name is DAP.

Superphosphate: This type of phosphate has been found in a number of rocks in India. Two rock phosphates — 'Musouri Phos' and 'Purulia Phos' are marketed as fertilizers. Rock phosphate is very useful for acid soils, because it contains more calcium. Its phosphates become soluble in acids. Therefore it should not be used in alkaline soils. Plants can absorb the total amount of the phosphate from rock phosphates. Besides, some trace elements are also available.

Muriate of potash: It contains 80-85 per cent of potassium chloride and 15-20 per cent of common salt. Its potash content is very high. Although it contains common salt (sodium chloride, NaCl) still it is useful for mum culture. Because chrysanthemum and dahlia, unlike the rose, are salt tolerant.

Sulphate of potash: It contains 50-54 per cent of pure potash (K_2O). Sulphate of potash becomes easily soluble in water and is readily absorbed by plants, and not easily leached out from the soil. The sulphate of potash produced in India is used as a laboratory chemical. For its use as a fertilizer it is imported from other countries. For growing quality tobacco sulphate of potash is essential. Hence the whole of the imported material is distributed in the tobacco growing area.

Sources of other nutrients

	Percentage (%)
Calcium	
Limestone	40
Quicklime	71
Slaked lime (air-slaked)	54
Plaster of Paris	23
Superphosphate	19
Dolomite (a form of lime)	30
Magnesium	
Dolomite	21
Magnesium sulphate	20
(also known as Mag sulf or Epsom salt)	
Sulphur	
Ammonium sulphate	24
Gypsum (Plaster of Paris)	18
Superphosphate	8-13
Boron	
Borax	11
Boric acid	14
Iron	
Iron sulphate	20
Manganese	
Manganese sulphate	36
Manganous oxide	77
Molybdenum	
Sodium molybdate	36
Zinc	
Zinc sulphate	36
Zinc oxide	79

8
Propagation

Chrysanthemum is widely propagated by seeds, suckers and shoot cuttings. The plants raised from seeds produce single or semi-double flowers. If vegetatively reproduced, i.e. grown from suckers and cuttings satisfactory blooms can be obtained.

Suckers

The production of suckers by the plant is a natural device by means of which the plant is easily and widely multiplied. Every plant puts forth a number of suckers on maturity. From a single well-grown plant 10-50 suckers can be obtained. Every sucker on separation from the mother plant may grow into an independent plant.

Professional growers will sever the suckers from the mother plant as soon as they will raise their heads 5-7 cm above the soil and transplant in a bed. It will induce the stool to produce more suckers. In the plains the plants send out suckers when the flowers fade out. The amateurs should select only the short and healthier suckers for growing more mother plants for the supply of cuttings in June and July. For growing exhibition blooms cuttings are preferable to suckers. The plants grown from suckers become hardy and vigorous, and produce medium-sized flowers. The suckers are indispensable for growing standards to produce numerous blooms.

After flowering the tops are pruned. The plant in this stage is called 'stool'. To get more suckers the stools are looked after with watering, manuring and plant protection measures.

For planting the suckers are detached with a sharp knife from near the point of sprouting. The small suckers may not have their roots. They should be planted in the sand medium inserting the etiolated (blanched) portion which has not developed chlorophyll. They will root like the cutting but very early, i.e. within a few days. The loss or absence of chlorophyll is a prerequisite for root emergence. The shoot portion of the plant develops chlorophyll as it is exposed to the sun. On the contrary the subterranean part that grows away from the sun remains blanched. Any root if exposed due to erosion develops chlorophyll. The tubers of potato are blanched. But if any of them peeps through the soil it becomes green due to exposure to the sun. But only the exposed portion develops chlorophyll. The green cuttings after insertion begin to lose chlorophyll from the portion that remains covered by sand. The application of root hormone tends to destroy the chlorophyll.

Cuttings

Chrysanthemums are multiplied more easily by means of shoot cuttings. The cuttings root throughout the year thus making its propagation more simplified. Before taking cuttings the selection of stocks is indispensable when a good result is aimed at. Owing to the infection of virus and eelworms good varieties are found to deteriorate. On the other hand partial mutations may take place in plants which may improve the variety. Therefore you should examine the stocks when it is in a full bloom condition. The plants bearing good flowers should be carefully labelled so as to denote their quality when blooming is over. Next to the selection of stocks comes the selection of young shoots for cuttings. Because the good cuttings always show a good percentage of rooting under a

Fig. 2: A good cutting

favourable condition. Moreover a good cutting grows to a good plant to produce quality blooms through scientific culture. How to perpetuate a plant exhausted after flowering for producing a number of good shoots for cuttings has been elaborately dealt with in the chapter entitled 'Care of Stools'.

The shoots with long internodes from the apical parts of the stool should not be preferred. The shoots with short internode from the basal parts of the stock are best. Too hard or too soft cuttings should not be chosen because they hardly turn to satisfaction. The commercial propagators do not discriminate as they use all the available shoots for cuttings.

Make the cuttings 5-7 cm long with lower end cut across 3 mm below a leaf-joint. Remove 1 or 2 leaves near the base. Immerse the base of the cuttings in water to moisten. This will facilitate to stick hormone powder to it. Then dip the base of the cutting (1cm) in hormone powder. To remove the excess powder tap the cutting lightly on the rim of the container. After 5 minutes insert the cuttings in sand medium just as the small seedlings are planted. To do this make holes 15 mm deep by a wooden prick at a distance of 5-6 cm. Insert one cutting in each hole and press the sand to tighten the base. Water with a water-can having its fine rose.

Fig. 3: Treating the cutting with root hormone before inserting into sand medium

Root hormone

Auxins are root promoting chemicals. They are available as indole acetic acid, indole butyric acid etc. The proprietary products in different trade names are available in the market. Of them Seradix of May and Baker is very popular. But at present it is not available. Many substitutes prepared by different producers are being sold in the market. They are not always dependable as their producers have not introduced quality control for maintaining the standard of their products. As such commercial propagators find it useful to prepare their own products.

Sand medium

Fine sand is preferable to coarse sand. Vermiculite may be used instead of sand. As a container for the growing medium shallow clay pots of 30 cm diameter which are known as "seed pans" are preferable. To prevent the disease infection both pot and medium should be sterilized. The sand should preferably be sieved to remove the grits. Obviously the pots must have the drain holes which should be more than one. All the holes should be properly crocked before filling with sand so that surplus water is drained out readily. Before inserting the cuttings soak the sand thoroughly.

Aftercare

The pots with cuttings should be protected from the direct sun and shower. So they should be placed in shed where there is plenty of diffused light and circulated air. If the fresh air is not circulated the rotting disease will occur resulting in the loss of cuttings before rooting. In a very humid atmosphere watering may not be required. Water the cutting pans only when it is needed. The excess moisture tends to cause disease incidence. The leaves of the cuttings may flag at noon. Because due to the rise in temperature the loss of water through leave pores (stomata) takes place immensely. To compensate it the rootless cuttings cannot absorb water from the rooting medium. To prevent it cover the pan with a piece of cloth moistened with water for five hours from 10 A.M. to 3 P.M. To keep it moist spray water over the cloth at an interval of 1-2 hours. It is a good sign if the flagging during the day is corrected at night. After six days the cuttings are likely to absorb more water which is evident from the leaf tissues that remain turgid even at the hot noon.

The hardy varieties root early, e.g. 'Casa Grande' which roots within a week in a favourable condition. On the contrary, the delicate varieties root within 2-3 weeks. The propagator should use separate pans for the hardy and delicate varieties.

Pricking out

On rooting the leaves of the cuttings will look fresh and tips growing. Just before pricking out water the pan copiously which will facilitate lifting without any root injury. Hold the top leaves with two fingers and pull out the cuttings from the sand.

First the rooted cuttings should be planted in thumb pots for a week or so. The potting compost to be used is as follows:

Heavy loam	10	litre
Leafmould	2	litre
Hoof and hornmeal	250	g
Superphosphate	150	g
Wood ash	100	g
Magnesium sulphate	50	g
Chalk dust	25	g

Mix loam, leafmould and chalk dust thoroughly. Leave the mixture in a pile in moist condition for a month. Then mix the other ingredients with the soil mixture and pile the compost and keep it moist for a month. Now this potting compost should be pulverized and sieved through 3 mm mesh before use.

Seeds

For raising new cultivars chrysanthemums, like dahlia, are grown from seeds. Chrysanthemum seeds, like the rose and dahlia, are hybrid in nature. Because the plants grown from seeds differ in characters of their mother. The seeds raised from the purposeful crossing are likely to produce the varieties of improved quality. A chapter exclusively for hybridizing has been included.

Seeds are small and hard-coated. A flower-head may produce a good number of seeds. The seeds raised in March are preserved in a dry condition for four months. In July they are sown in a sterilized seed compost. The following compost may be used for this purpose:

Coarse sand	5	litre
Leafmould	5	litre
Superphosphate	100	g

Hoof and hornmeal	250 g
Muriate of potash	100 g

The ingredients should be mixed thoroughly and heaped in a moist condition for a month. Then pulverize and sieve this compost. Now fill the seed pan with the compost as usual. To sterilize the compost treat it with the solution of formalin (40 ml/l). Drench the compost with the solution and cover the pans with a polythene sheet for 48 hours. Then remove the cover to let the formalin gas escape. After a week seed should be sown in the compost as usual. On sowing cover the seeds with the same sterilized compost. The cover should not exceed 5 mm in thickness. Then water once a day as usual. The seeds germinate within 2-3 weeks. From the seed pans the seedlings should be transferred when they are in the stage of 4-6 leaves. The compost to be used is the same as recommended for potting the rooted cuttings in the thumb pots.

9
Potting Compost

For growing good chrysanthemums enriched potting compost with balanced nutrients is essential. Not only that, desired texture and structure of the compost are also needed. The potting compost is used in July and August. But one should start producing it right from February. The work is done in two stages. In the first phase soil, humus and lime are mixed and heaped. In the later stage the fertilizer mix is added to the soil-humus mixture.

First stage

Heavy loam	10 buckets (10 litre capacity)
Humus (leafmould/cowmanure)	4 buckets
Chalk dust	150 g

Mix the chalk dust with the soil, then humus is added to it. Keep the mix in a heap which must be in a moist condition. It must be protected from showers. To keep the heap moist watering is needed at an interval of two weeks. The heap should be covered with a polythene sheet or tarpaulin. One should be careful to see that no weed grows on the heap. This will eliminate the eelworms from the compost heap. Because eelworms cannot live for a long time without plants. During the rains eelworms destroy the leaf tissues of chrysanthemum, consequently the infested leaves are destroyed as done by the fungous disease. At an interval of 50-60 days the heap should be cut with a spade and piled again as before. This is done to cause aeration which is needed for normal activities of the soil microbes.

Second stage

The fertilizer should be mixed with the compost* by the middle of May. Any of the following mixtures can be used with advantage for 10 buckets (10 litre capacity) of compost.

1

Hoof and hornmeal	5 kg
Bonemeal	1500 g
Wood ash	1500 g
Magnesium sulphate	250 g

2

Fishmeal	3 kg
Bonemeal	1500 g
Wood ash	1500 g
Magnesium sulphate	250 g

3

Oilcake (Neem/Mustard/Groundnut)	3 kg
Bonemeal	1500 g
Wood ash	150 g
Magnesium sulphate	250 g

4

Bloodmeal	2 kg
Bonemeal	1500 g
Wood ash	1500 g
Magnesium sulphate	250 g

*Loam, humus and chalk.

5

Fishmeal	1 kg
Bloodmeal	500 g
Hoof and hornmeal	2 kg
Bonemeal	1500 g
Wood ash	1500 g
Magnesium sulphate	250 g

6

Oilcake (*Neem*/Mustard/Groundnut/Castor)	2 kg
Hoof and hornmeal/Fishmeal	2 kg
Superphosphate	2 kg
Muriate of potash	1 kg
Magnesium sulphate	250 g

7

Urea	1 kg
Hoof and hornmeal	2 kg
Superphosphate	2 kg
Muriate of potash	1 kg
Magnesium sulphate	250 g

8

Floramix/Sterameal/Rallimeal	2500 g
Magnesium sulphate	250 g

Oilcake should be pulverized before use. Hoof and hornmeal is available in different grades. The material of any grade which is available can be used. For mixing spread the compost on the floor. Then the fertilizer mixture is spread over it. Mix the whole by cutting the heap with a spade. Then sieve the mix through 5 mm mesh. For decomposition of the organic substances keep the mix in a moist condition for a month in a heap. This compost is meant for the second and the final shifts. For potting in thumb pots and 9 cm pots the potting compost has been mentioned separately at the proper places.

10
Shifting

In the different stages of growth chrysanthemum should be shifted to pots of different dimensions to ensure a desirable growth. I am often asked by the amateurs as to the usefulness of this operation. They cannot make out that by this method a check can be imparted to the vegetative growth of a plant resulting in a good flower production. The judicious control over food and space in the different stages of growth makes the plants preserve energy for a good crop of flowers.

When well rooted and the apical growth is started the cuttings become fit for shifting. First they should be potted in thumb pots. After a week they should be potted in 9 cm pots. This shifting is known as "first potting". The grower should be careful not to neglect this operation. It is not good if they directly shift a small cutting into a large pot. This cultural operation, I am sure, is very important specially when an exhibition bloom is aimed at. I hope the readers would carefully follow the instructions laid down here to appreciate the utility of and gain experience about this cultural operation.

Most amateurs cannot shift their mums for several times, because of the limitation of their time and resources. My suggestion to them with regard to shifting is that they should at least shift their cuttings twice—first into the 9 cm pots and then finally into 22 cm pots.

Now a question arises: how long a rooted cutting will be allowed to grow in a 9 cm pot? It is significant no doubt. When the roots will begin to crowd in the space between the pot wall and compost, and the growth will be retarded it is then that the plant will be fit for the second shift. Now again another problem crops up: how one can be able to examine the root growth? The retardation of the apical growth may be caused due to some other reasons. So it is imperative to examine the root growth when the apical growth is retarded. It can be done simply by knocking out the plant from the pot as illustrated in Fig. 4.

Fig. 4: Knocking out the plant from the pot for testing its root growth

The second shift should be made into the 15 cm pots and the final shift should be made into 22 cm pots. In case of the final shift the same principle of testing the root growth has to be followed. It deserves to be mentioned here that there are some robust varieties that require larger pots for their vigorous growth. Mainly some American varieties are of this type. This consideration should be made at the stage of final shifting. Either the pots for the third shift should be slightly bigger, say 25 cm or a fourth shift may be made into the 25 cm pot.

11

Shape and Size of the Pots

There may be some controversies as regards the shape and size of the pots suitable for growing chrysanthemums. However every school will agree that there are three aspects of the utility of a flower pot. The first thing is the appearance, the second is to provide enough space suitable for root growth. The third being the presence of the drain holes. The experience shows that the side holes are better in many respects. The method of crocking in this case has been shown in Fig. 5.

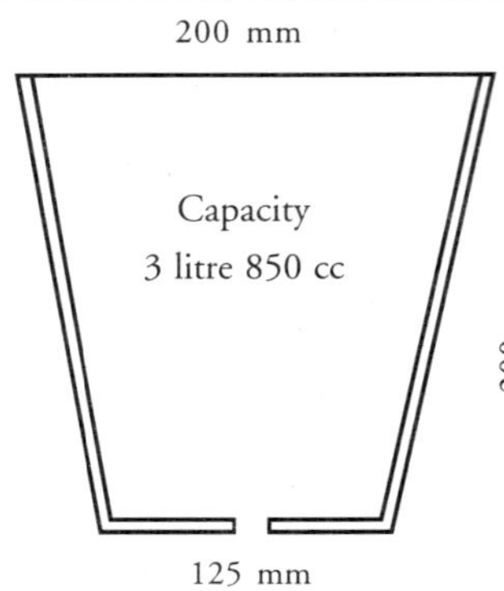

Fig. 5: Size and shape of the pot

In this age of plastics we are fortunate enough to have polythene flower pots. They are good in many respects. Firstly, they are unbreakable and last normally a lifetime. Secondly, due to the nonporousness of the substance evaporation through the body of a pot does not arise thus saving labour for watering to a great extent. Thirdly, they can be easily cleaned and sterilized. This merit is not of little worth so far as the disease infection is concerned. Fourthly, it maintains soil at 4 or 5°F higher than that of earthen pots. So it is more useful in a cold weather. Lastly, it is preferred due to the lightness of the substance.

12
Potting

As explained earlier the rooted cuttings will be ready for the first shift into 9 cm pots after they have grown in thumb pots for 10-15 days. The size of the pot should be 9 cm, i.e. both the diameter and the depth of the pot will be 9 cm. The capacity of a pot of this size should be 270 cc.

First potting

To prepare a suitable compost for the first potting is a very important thing that needs a careful attention. It should not be rich in comparison with that to be used for the subsequent shifts. The composition is as follows:

Heavy loam	1 bucket (10 litre capacity)
Humus	2 litre
Hoof and hornmeal	200 g
Superphosphate	200 g
Muriate of potash	100 g
Magnesium sulphate	25 g
Chalk dust	20 g

Mix the ingredients thoroughly and heap the mixture in a moist condition for a week before use. Clean your pots by washing and then sterilize by dipping them into formalin solution for 5 minutes. To make the solution add 400 cc formalin to a bucket of water (10 litre capacity). The treated pots should be kept covered by a polythene sheet for 48 hours. Then they can be used for potting. For sterilization of the potting compost see 'Soil Sterilization'.

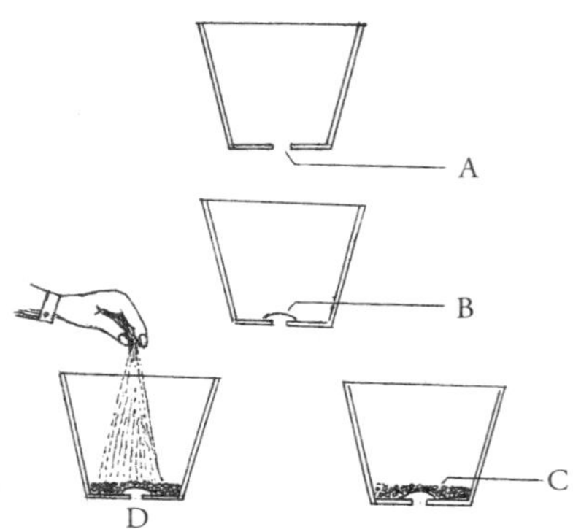

Fig. 6: Crocking
A - Drain hole
B - Crock with convex side upwards
C - Layer of grit over the crock
D - Sprinkling dry sand over the layer of grit

Next comes crocking. This operation is also very important (Fig. 6). Place a piece of broken pot on the bottom hole with the concave side downwards. And then cover the crock with a layer of grit obtained from sieving sand. Now to fill up the voids in the layer of grits sprinkle very dry sand over it which will go downwards to occupy the gaps between the grits. If the pot has side holes shut the hole with a piece of broken pot placing it vertically and then cover the crock with a heap of grit (Fig. 7).

Now fill the pot with the compost upto 4 cm from the bottom and press down with fingers. Remove the thumb pot and place the root ball on the compost of the pot and fill it with the compost which should be pressed down with fingers holding the cutting vertically. Leave a space of one centimetre empty from the top for watering. Water the plants with the fine rose of a water-can (Fig. 13). Keep the pots in shade for 3-5 days until the root growth is started.

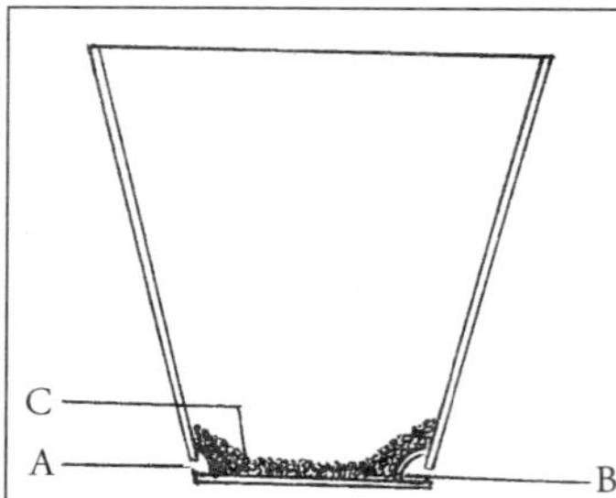

Fig. 7: Side drain holes
A - Hole B - Crock C - Grit

Owing to the porousness of the earthen pots evaporation takes place very rapidly in a dry weather through their bodies. Thus the soil of a small pot becomes dry quickly, which is definitely harmful to the normal growth. The remedial measure can be taken by inserting the pots upto the rim in a sand bed (Fig. 8).

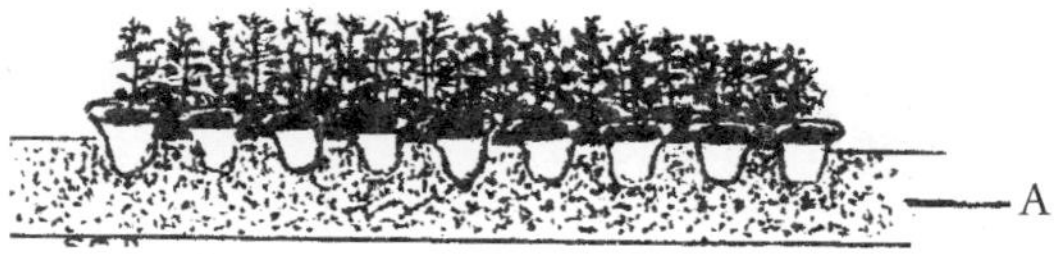

Fig. 8: Thumb pots are inserted into sand bed
A - Sand bed

The potted cuttings should be kept in a place away from the full sun for a few days until the root growth is resumed.

Second potting

Fig. 9: Ramming

A plant should stay only for 3-4 weeks in a 9 cm pot. Its root growth should be examined by knocking it out from the pot in order to determine if it is ready for the next potting. The size of the pot should be 15 cm for this shift. The compost recommended in chapter entitled 'Potting Compost' should be used for this shift.

Cleaning, sterilizing and crocking a pot should be as in the case of the previous potting. The pots collected from the potter's shop need not be sterilized. Fill a pot upto one-third of its depth with the potting compost. For pressing down the compost use a rammer to make the soil considerably hard. Prepare a wooden rammer with one end blunt and the other pointed for this purpose (Fig. 9). After ramming the compost upto the lower third of the pot take the plant out of the 9 cm pot. Remove the grits and crocks from the root ball and place it on the compost

Fig. 10: Ramming

holding the plant vertically. Then fill in the sides of the root ball and ram carefully with the pointed end of the rammer so that the roots are not damaged (Fig. 10). Now complete the operation by filling in the rest of the pot and ramming with the blunt head of the rammer. This time also leave one centimetre of space empty for watering. For the sake of neatness in appearance use a little finely sieved compost on the top. Then water with the fine rose of a can. After potting the pots should be placed in a sunny situation.

Final potting

The 20 cm pots are normally used for the final potting. A plant takes nearly two months to be ready for this shift after the second potting. You should, however, examine your plants to be sure that they need more food and space.

The same compost should be used as for the second potting. The cleaning, sterilizing and crocking should be done as in the case of previous pottings. Ram down the soil upto ¼ of the depth of the pot. Place the root ball on the firm base of the compost holding the plant vertically. For the rest follow the same procedure as for the second potting.

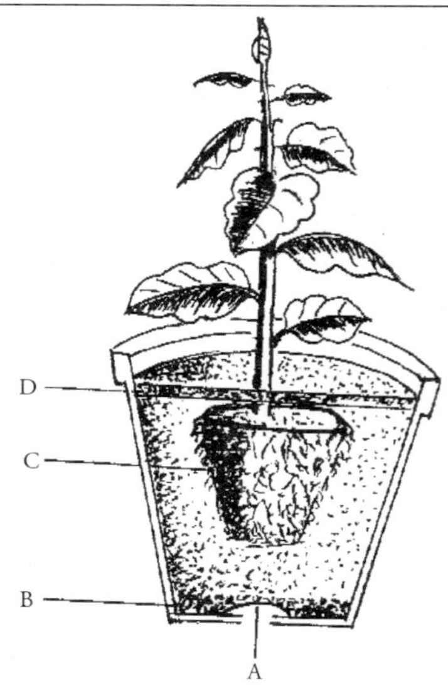

Fig. 11: Shifting (final potting)

A - Crock B - Layer of grit
C - Root ball of previous potting
D - Mulch

13
Staking

The chrysanthemum stems are weak that need support against the wind, especially when the tops become heavy with blooms. The staking is generally required just after the final shift. The strong slender canes of a bamboo or reed, one for each stem, should be inserted deeply near the base of the plant. Primarily they should be a little longer than those usually required so that the height can be adjusted to that of the plant including the length of the stalk of the flower. When the buds begin to bloom the extra height of the canes should be removed by shearing. Care should be taken to see that the canes do not shelter any insect in their damaged tissues. Get the stems tied loosely with twines to the respective canes (Fig. 12). It should be borne in mind that staking should never affect a good display. This is why the art of staking is a thing to be learnt with an aesthetic aptitude. To camouflage the stake it should be light green in colour. For this purpose dip the stakes in water colour solution for a few hours before use. But any paint should not be

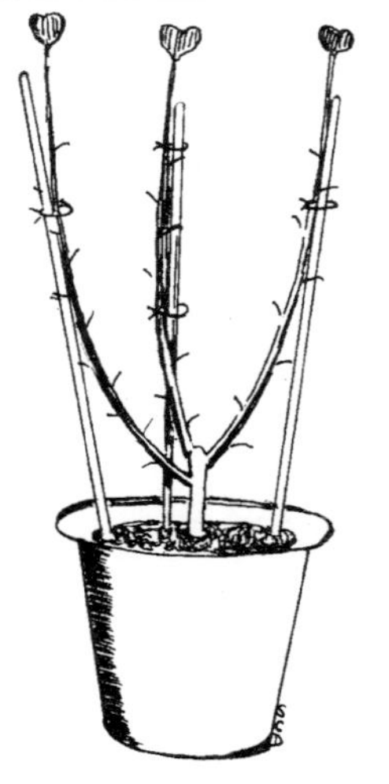

Fig. 12: Staking
Leaves are not shown to make it distinct

used. Because it will make the stakes glossy thus making them distinct from other greens beside it.

As luxuriant foliage growth attracts insects, so birds are attracted to your plants in search of prey. They like your good friend destroy the insects. But at the same time they may behave unfriendly by breaking the tender twigs of your valuable plants. Would you ever like to allow them to do this sort of harm to your plants? Black nylon cords may be strung overhead in several lines to discourage the birds to frequent your garden.

14
Watering

Judicious watering is not an easy task, so far as chrysanthemum culture is concerned. Proper watering complying with the need of the plant is an essential factor leading to success. The relative humidity and temperature of the atmosphere are regarded as the important factors controlling the amount of water needed by the plants. The plants with more foliage obviously need more water. Because with the increase of the transpiring surface more water escapes as vapour through the stomata of leaves.

Tapping chrysanthemum pots with a tapper helps determine when our plants need watering. A piece of wood, say 8 cm x 5 cm x 5 cm fixed to a long cylindrical handle of a can at right angles will serve the purpose of a tapper. Tap your pots gently holding the handle of the tapper. If they emit a dull sound watering should be withheld.

Fig. 13: Watering with a fine rose of the

In Europe and America the gardeners use moisture meter to determine the water need of the pot plants. It is a small stick-like instrument that has a digital scale for reading. On touching the soil of the pot the meter reading will indicate if watering is needed. If this sort of instrument is introduced in this country the chrysanthemum grower will be benefited.

During the hot months of the year the transpiration takes place at a very high rate. Specially at noon the amount of water transpired through the stomata is greater than that absorbed by the plant. Hence the leaves droop. The flagging of leaves and tender shoots at summer noon can be effectively checked by overhead spraying of cold water.

Always use rose with the can for watering your potted chrysanthemums. When watering the plants in 9 cm pots a very fine rose should be used. The most important thing with regard to watering is to determine when a plant needs water. The leaves and the tender shoots begin to lose their turgid appearance in scarcity of water. This is a good indicator that helps determine the time of watering.

As the soil of the chrysanthemum pots is rammed it is found to absorb water very slowly. Fill the empty space completely with water, when it percolates fill again as before until the excess water drips through the drain hole.

124. 'SEATONS SULPHUR' (Quilled).

126. 'CHRISTMAS CRYSTAL' (Spider). Courtesy: Basab Datta

125. 'GLORIO DEO' (Reflexed). Courtesy: Basab Datta

127. 'ALFRED SIMPSON' (Incurving). Courtesy: Basab Datta

152. 'BOLA-DE-ORO' (Incurved).

153. A bronze spider.

154. White sport of "KEN-ROKU-KANGIKU' (Incurved).

155. 'KOKKA SHOZON' (Incurved). Courtesy: Subrata Goswami

On the next page

156. 'ROYAL PURPLE' (Spider) (top).

157. 'PETER MAY' (Reflexed) (bottom). (Photo: Author)

158. 'KEN-ROKU-KANGIKU' (Incurved).

15
Stopping and Timing

The new entrants in the field of chrysanthemum culture are generally confused with the terms STOPPING AND TIMING. With a view to removing this confusion great care has been taken here to interpret the terms as lucidly as possible with the help of a suitable illustration (Fig. 14).

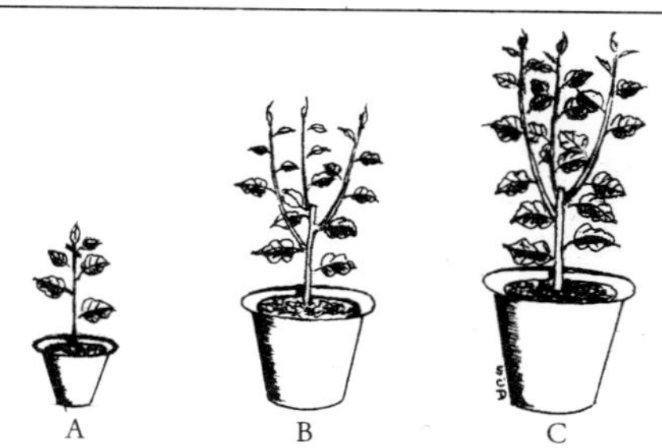

Fig. 14: Stopping
A - Cutting stopped by pinching
B - Laterals are growing
C - Three laterals for three crown buds

When a bud appears at the apex of the shoot the apical growth is checked naturally and side shoots or laterals begin to develop at the axils or leaf-joints. This first bud that appears naturally, i.e. without any forcing, is known as the 'Break Bud' (Fig. 16). It starves practically if laterals are allowed to grow. Those laterals will also terminate with a bud which is known as the 'First Crown Bud'. When a first crown bud appears the laterals are also thrown out from the axils which in their turn produce buds that are known as 'Second Crown Buds'. The third crown buds are also produced in the same manner, but they are termed as 'Terminal Buds'. Because when the terminal buds appear the leaf-joints instead of throwing branches develop buds around the central terminal one thus indicating the end or termination of the growth of the plant (Fig. 15).

Fig. 15: Terminal buds indicating the termination of vegetative growth

The growers should know that the break buds are generally removed; because they open when the plant is still young. If you want the first crown bud to flower then remove all the new shoots developed from the axils. The second crown buds are also left to flower in the same way. But in case of the terminal buds thin out the cluster of buds leaving the central bigger one to flower. Not only that, the buds that appear from the leaf-joints should also be removed.

'Timing' is meant for coinciding the blooming with the show date. For timing the stopping is to be done. For a single-stem system the planting date should be fixed accordingly. Suppose the 25th December is fixed for your local flower show date. You should start growing abiding by the following programme for a large-flowered variety (previously known as 'Japanese Chrysanthemum'):

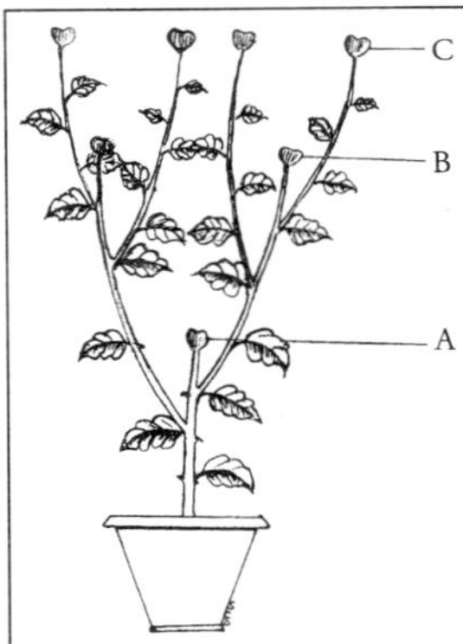

Fig. 16: Bud diagram

A - Break bud
B - First crown bud
C - Second crown bud

1st potting on the 29th July
2nd potting on the 22nd August
Final potting on the 14th September.

The break bud will appear on the 25th October, which will bloom on the 25th December, the local show date.

The tender plants are stopped by pinching the tip with a view to delaying the blooming and securing a number of shoots for more flowers. Therefore for timing, i.e. securing blooms on the fixed show date, the stopping may be necessary. To raise blooms from the first crown buds stop the plant after two weeks of second potting. If the show is held late in the season the blooms have to be raised from the second crown buds. For this you should stop the shoots developed after the first stopping. It should be borne in mind that a period of 90 days is elapsed between the first stopping and the date of blooming. For flowering of the second crown bud a period of 80 days is needed after the second stopping.

It is however to be remembered that the interval of time noted above is for its extensive use. Because it is likely to differ owing to the varietal and climatic peculiarities. A skilful practice of timing depends entirely upon the growers' experience as to the individual characteristics of the different varieties and local climatic conditions. That is why when a new variety is introduced the ambitious growers arrange for the trial with those varieties before aiming at placing their blooms in a flower show.

16

Disbudding

The removal of the flower bud is called disbudding. Usually the flower buds appear more than what is wanted. Therefore the selected buds should be retained for blooming and the others be removed. For the large blooms 'one bloom per shoot' is the rule, that should be the central one which appears first. Obviously the lateral buds must be removed. On the contrary the central bud is removed if spray-type blooming is required. This is adopted in case of the pompons. The large-flowered varieties are also produced in the spray form, especially when such a variety, say SPRAY MUMS, is included in the show schedule.

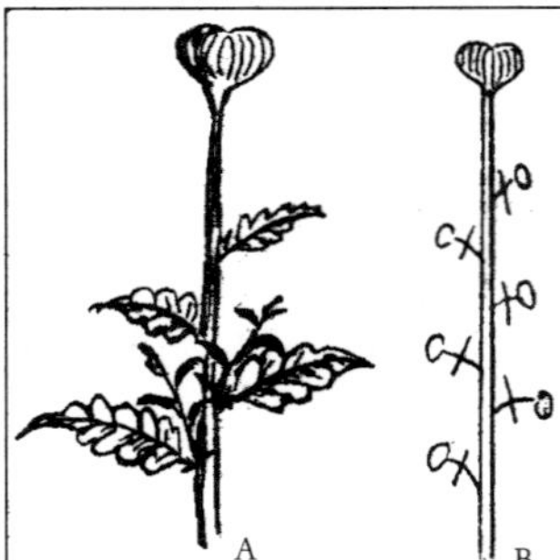

Fig. 17: Disbranching and disbudding

A - Shoots below the bud are removed

B - Lateral buds below the terminal bud are removed

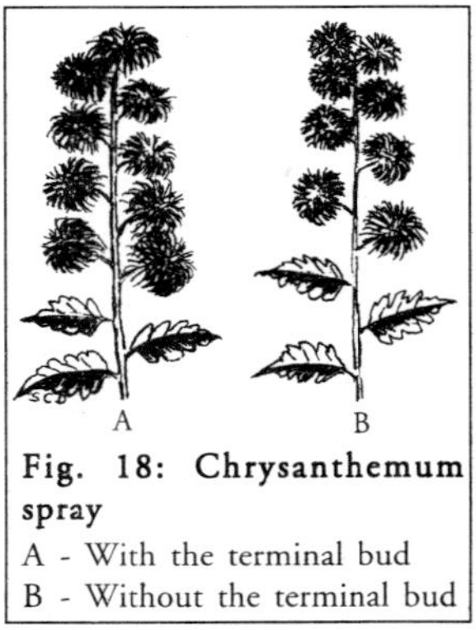

Fig. 18: Chrysanthemum spray

A - With the terminal bud

B - Without the terminal bud

Pinch out the buds to be rejected in the early stage. Care should be taken not to cause any injury to the selected buds and the flower stalks.

17
Desuckering

The sucker growth must be checked, otherwise the energy will be diverted in the form of the flow of nutrition. As soon as the growths will raise their heads above the mulch sever them from the point of their origin. If they have developed roots they may be treated as new plants. If not, they can be treated as etiolated cuttings which on inserting in the rooting medium will root earlier than usual. If the base of the cutting loses chlorophyll and becomes blanch, this is regarded as the prerequisite condition of rooting. The cuttings having blanched base are called etiolated cuttings.

18
Mulching

The mulch prevents hardening of the surface layer of the pot soil exposed to sun and air. The baked soil has to be forked in or it will gradually be impervious to water. Forking at a short interval injures the feeder roots again and again, which crowd near the surface.

Spread coarse manure in a layer of 1-2 cm thickness over the surface. Care should be taken when watering so that the mulching material is not disturbed, i.e. remains in the uniform thickness. The mulching with a mixture of leafmould and cowmanure is considered better than cowmanure alone. For feeding top dressing or liquid manure can be applied on the mulch when necessary. When the mulch gets decomposed and mixed with the soil put mulch again as before. Mulch conserves moisture of the pot soil. So less watering is needed (Fig. 19).

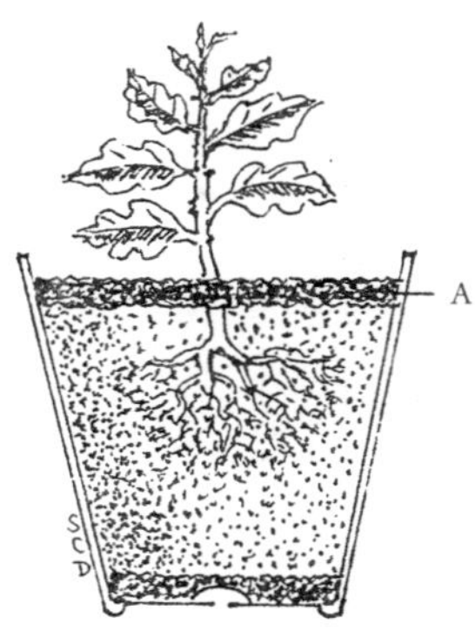

Fig. 19: Vertical section of a pot with the plant

A - Mulch

19
Soil Aeration

Growing roots need oxygen for respiration which makes them active to absorb more nutrients. The useful soil microbes that change ammonia into nitrates also need aeration. In the soil mass between the soil particles numerous pores exist. They remain filled with either water or air. Just after watering the pores are filled with water, so air comes out. As soon as the water is absorbed by the plants the pore spaces are occupied again by air. In this process the soil pores are occupied alternately by air and water which is a useful process for the good growth of the plants. If the watering is judicious aeration is not affected. When water runs short the leaves and growing shoots begin to wilt. For good aeration watering should be done just before wilting.

The pots of burnt clay have numerous pores in their body. Air enters through those pores. Not only that the evaporation of soil moisture takes place through those pores also. The roots are found to crowd to form a mat adjacent to the pot wall. This is due to the fact that roots get more air in this region, which enters through the pores of the wall.

20

Height Control by Chemicals

The exhibition bloom on a comparatively short plant is very decorative. If flowering is delayed the plant grows tall. Dr. W.M. Chapman writes (1959), "if grown early 'Madonna' grows to about 8 feet, it will certainly give its grower plenty of exercise." Not only 'Madonna' there are many other varieties also which can grow to 8 feet. Secondly, the use of chemical nitrogen such as urea, ammonium sulphate, calcium ammonium nitrate etc. makes the plants quick growing. The plants having long internodes become taller. The chemical nitrogen however makes the bloom larger if applied after the appearance of buds. But if applied early the flower stalk will be longer. The excessive use of nitrogen makes the petals soft which will wither early.

The use of chemicals to control the height of chrysanthemum is becoming popular to the showmen. In the shows the short plants having large blooms are winning the prizes. Hence the significance. There are three chemicals which are used for this purpose. They are B-Nine, Phosphon-D and Cycocel.

B-Nine: The use of B-9 has been dealt with in the Chrysanthemum Manual of the National Chrysanthemum Society (England). Another article entitled 'Effect of B-9 on Flower Longevity and Vegetative Growth' appears in the Proceedings of the American Society of Horticultural Science, Vol. 91, page 645.

B-9 is also known as 'Alar-85'. It is applied by spraying on foliage. The requisite concentration being 2,500 ppm. The foliage tissue must be turgid but the surface be dry. After stopping when the laterals grow to 3-4 cm long apply the chemical. To shorten the flower stalk apply again when the flower bud is selected for blooming. Spraying during the period of short days is efficacious. The application after the second week of August is found fruitful.

Cycocel: It is used by spraying on foliage and also by drenching soil.

Phosphon-D: It is applied as a soil drench.

These chemicals are not easily available in this country. These may be available with the firms which supply chemicals to the research or institutional laboratories.

21
Sufficiency vs Deficiency of Nutrients and Feeding

Chrysanthemum needs nitrogen in larger quantities. The soil particles cannot adsorb nitrate ions. Hence it is fleeing. A large portion of it goes down through leaching with percolating water, and a portion escapes as gaseous ammonia from the soil. So in the feeding process it has to be replenished at a regular interval.

Nutrients

Nitrogen: The luxuriant vegetative growth of chrysanthemum is mainly due to the large quantities of nitrogen absorbed by the plant. Nitrogen is responsible for the growth of green vegetative parts. The large green leaves and long internodes are due to the large quantities of nitrogen.

The deficiency of nitrogen is first indicated by the pale green to yellow colour of the leaves. Gradually the growing leaves and stems become smaller and smaller as deficiency increases. In general the shortage of nitrogen makes the plant stunted in growth.

Phosphorus: The chrysanthemum, like most plants, needs plenty of phosphorus (but less than nitrogen) for its stronger growth. Nitrogen makes the growth soft and sappy, but phosphorus makes it hard and strong. The strong growth can resist many fungous diseases. Phosphorus makes the roots stronger that become capable of absorbing more nutrients. As it causes early maturity flower buds come up early. For producing quality blooms for exhibition the plant must not suffer from the want of this element. The flower stalk must be strong enough to hold the bloom upright. This can be achieved by supplementing phosphorous fertilizers.

The phosphorus deficiency is indicated by the dark bluish green colour of the leaves, thin stalks, small leaves, limited lateral growths, delayed maturity and premature defoliation. The flowers may droop because of soft stalks.

Potassium: It is the third member of the Big Three—nitrogen, phosphorus and potash. The rapid growth made by nitrogen is due to the rapid multiplication of cells. These cells must be filled up with carbohydrates and other synthesised products. The role of potash is to build up these products. Potash, like phosphorus, causes early maturity and makes the wood hard and strong. In summer when much loss of water takes place by transpiration through leaf pores (stomata), potash saves the plants by inhibiting the process of transpiration. Chrysanthemums have an affinity for potash. It is the only element which is absorbed more than its requirements. Potassium is very helpful to enhance the disease resistant quality. Premature loss of leaves, drying up of margins of leaves are the symptoms of deficiency of potash. Flowers may droop because of soft stalks. The colour of blooms may be dull.

Magnesium: It makes the leaves glossy green. The colour of blooms also becomes brighter. Magnesium, like nitrogen, is leached out from the soil easily. Hence the deficiency of the element is a common occurrence.

The magnesium deficiency is exhibited by the yellowish colour (chlorosis) of the leaves.

Iron: The deficiency of iron causes poor colouring of flowers and yellowing of leaves. Iron sulphate (Fe_2SO_4) is applied in the soil to remove the iron deficiency in the plants. By spraying foliar feed containing iron salts the deficiency of the element can be removed.

Boron: Boron is a very important element for growing good flowers. It makes the white blooms very attractive. Its deficiency is likely to occur in an alkaline soil, where boric acid (H_3BO_3) should be applied at the rate of 3 grams per litre of water. Three litres of such solution is sufficient for five pots. It must be borne in mind that boron even in a slight overdose will kill the plants.

Zinc: The length of the internodes is shortened accompanied by a rosetting or whorling of leaves.

Feeding

The manures and fertilizers used in preparing the potting compost cannot sustain the plant growth for a long time with the important food elements. However rich a soil may be certain elements are likely to run short before long. Of them nitrogen is most fleeing, especially in sandy soils. It is easily leached out thus going beyond the root zone of the plants. This is why nitrogen has to be replenished at short intervals during the growing period. In case of chrysanthemums without the deficiency symptoms nitrogen should not be used. The supplemental feed is applied in three ways, i.e. top dressing, liquid manure and foliar spray. Although basically the same they are applied in different ways.

Top dressing: Generally chemical fertilizers or a mixture of chemical or organic materials of nutritive value is used as top dressing. It is useful to ground plants as well as pot plants. A top dressing is applied after forking the soil round the plants and it must be followed by a good irrigation. It can be applied directly on the mulch, i.e. without forking the soil. Generally top dressings are needed at an interval of 4-8 weeks during the growing period. Any of the following mixtures is recommended for chrysanthemums:

1

Humus	1 bucket (10 litre capacity)
Hoof and hornmeal	500 g
Superphosphate	250 g
Sulphate of potash/Muriate of potash	100 g
Magnesium sulphate	50 g

2 (for 50 pots)

Humus	1 bucket (10 lt)
Bloodmeal	300 g
Fishmeal	400 g
Wood ash	300 g
Magnesium sulphate	50 g

3 (for each pot)

Floramix/Sterameal	15 g

4 (for 50 pots)

Humus	10 lt
Fishmeal	750 g
Muriate of potash	200 g
Magnesium sulphate	50 g

5 (for 50 pots)

Bloodmeal	750 g
Wood ash/Muriate of potash	200 g
Magnesium sulphate	50 g

Liquid manure: Feeding with liquid manure is very popular. Because it is quick acting and cheap. It can be used at an interval of 7-10 days; it is used in a very dilute form. A liquid manure should not be in a concentrated form.

Fresh cowdung, oilcake and fish are the main ingredients for preparing a liquid manure.

Fresh cowdung	1 kg
Oilcake (Mustard/groundnut)	250 g
Small fish (minor carps or fingerlings)	250 g
Water	5 lt

The above ingredients are mixed together and put in a bowl for decomposition. It will decompose and be ready for use within 10-

15 days. Before use get it more diluted by adding 10 litres of water. Now 50 grams of sulphate of potash and 25 grams of magnesium sulphate can be added to it. Water the pots 15 minutes before applying the manure. Use this diluted mixture in 50 pots. The liquid of such strength requires an interval of 2-3 weeks.

Foliar feeding: A plant can be fed through leaves. Certain nutrients due to complex soil reactions cannot be used by plants. To get rid of this trouble nutrient mixtures in a liquid form are straightaway applied on the leaves by spraying. Generally the trace elements or micro-nutrients are fed through leaves. The foliar feeds are of two types—some for the main elements and others for the trace elements. They are also used separately and should not be mixed together.

Nowadays proprietary products which can be used as foliar feed are available in the market. They should be used as per the directions of their manufacturers. A list of popular products is given below:

Products	*Producers*
Agromin	Arries Agrovet Industrial Products Ltd., Mumbai-43
Tracel-2	Rallis India Ltd., Bangalore-54
Multiplex	Karnatak Agro Chemicals, Bangalore-10
Micronutrient Mix	Pausak Ltd., Baroda-3
Vipul	Godrej Boecy
Trasco-5	Super Agro India, 22B, Satchasi Para Rd., Calcutta-2

22
Protection from Rains

To ensure a good result the plants should be protected from the rains. Chrysanthemums exposed to showers during the rains suffer from many troubles, such as eelworm attacks, fungous diseases like root rotting and leaf rotting, etc. The frequent showers or downpourings are definitely harmful whereas occasional showers are found to freshen the plants. In the region of clay soils these harmful elements are less active than those of the sandy soils of an arid zone.

As the plants need plenty of sunshine they cannot be placed under any ordinary shed. The polythene or fibre glass shed is suitable for this purpose. Nowadays U.V. stabilized polythene sheets are available in the market. This material lasts longer with its transparency. It is also known as 'greenhouse sheet'.

After the heavy downpour the plants when exposed to the sun wilt. It is due to spoiling of the rootlets that absorb water. This phenomenon is caused due to the attack of harmful soil fungi. If the protection by any transparent shed cannot be afforded the pots should be kept tilted until the deluge is over.

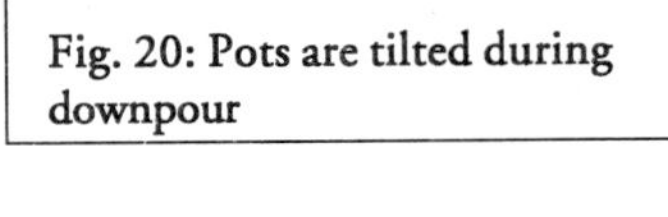

Fig. 20: Pots are tilted during downpour

The pompon type mums can stand continuous rains but the large-flowered types are very delicate, hence sensitive to rains. Therefore for the cut-flowers pompons are preferred most for growing in the ground under the sky.

23

Large Exhibition Mums on Single-Stem System

The large exhibition chrysanthemums were known as 'Japanese Chrysanthemums' until the fifth decade of the past century. The amateurs who cannot devote their time for a long period of culture may well resort to this method of growing for the large-flowered varieties. Nowadays chrysanthemums with an erect stem (or stems) are called 'Standard'. Because they grow erect like a tree.

An one-stem standard of the large exhibition type blooms within 4-5 months. If its blooming is required in the middle of December do the first potting in the middle of August. Generally no stopping is done. If it is imperative for timing pinch the tip as stated already. Amongst the laterals select only one to grow; obviously others should be nipped in the early stage. Stake the plant as usual. No laterals or sucker growths should be allowed. Other cultural methods and practices for the protection of blooms should be meticulously followed.

24
Multi-Stemmed Standards

This system of growing the large-flowered mums is widely practised. Generally 2-5 stems are grown by stopping the plant of the second potting. After stopping the required number of shoots are selected and allowed to grow. Obviously others will be pinched off. Other things of the cultural operations are the same as for the single-stem system.

25
Pot-Mums

A number of standards are grown in a pot of 20-25 cm diameter. Generally 5, 7 or 9 cuttings are potted at an equal distance. One of them at the centre and the remaining ones are planted along the periphery. The height of the plants should not exceed the height of the pot used to grow them. Usually they are grown as one-stem standards. But some prefer to grow them as double-stem standards by stopping as usual. In that case the number of blooms are doubled at the cost of the size of the blooms. Therefore one-stem standards for pot mums are preferable.

As regards the selection of varieties the dwarf varieties must be chosen. Their colour should be according to the specifications of the schedule of a particular show. They may be of the same colour or different colours. In the latter case two contrasting colours should be preferred. Their arrangement is shown in Fig. 21.

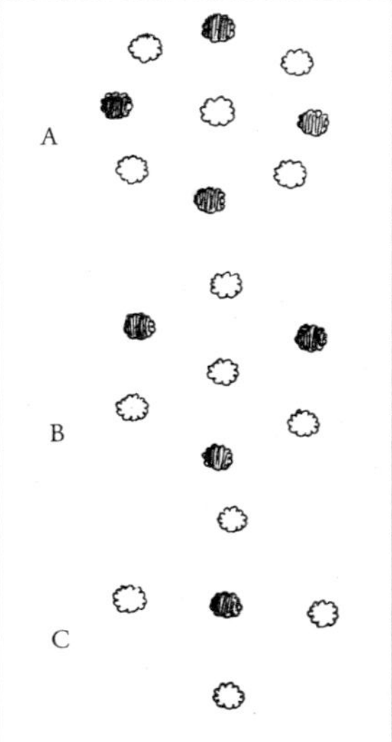

Fig. 21: Colour arrangements for pot-mums

A - 9 flowers of 2 different colours
B - 7 flowers of 2 different colours
C - 5 flowers of 2 different colours

To make it easy the cuttings of only a single variety are planted in a pot. Because the growing and flowering habits being the same the uniformity in all respects is brought about easily.

26
Mini-Mums

The 'mini-mums' are of two types—one with the pompons and the other with the large-flowered varieties. In both the cases very small pots, say 12 cm, are used. The size of the pot must conform to the specification as given in the schedule of a particular show. The height of the plant should not exceed 15 cm.

In case of the pompons one rooted cutting (not sucker) from a thumb pot will be potted in a 12 cm pot as usual. To make a thick, compact and symmetrical head first stop the cutting at the early stage and then pinch the shoots repeatedly.

For a large-flowered mini-mum a single-stem standard of a dwarf variety is grown in a 12 cm pot as usual. To make it easy take a shoot from the mother plant which has just shown its flower bud in September. Immediately after rooting transplant it directly in a 12 cm pot using the general potting compost; stake the plant as usual. Obviously the cutting will bear buds at a very early stage. Select the break bud for flowering. Other buds and laterals if any must be removed. With proper cultural operations especially with feeding a very large flower can be obtained from such small plants. The spider varieties grown for this purpose look very decorative, and in the market they can fetch a good price. I made an experiment with the cuttings in which the flower buds were just visible. The varieties which root early were selected. They produced good blooms to satisfaction.

27

Thousand Blooms per Plant

It is innovated by the Japanese and termed in their language as *"Sen Rin Tsukuri"*. A plant with its massive head is grown for numerous medium-sized blooms, just contrary to the pompons which produce small blooms. A large-flowered variety with a robust growing habit is selected for this purpose. Other varietal characteristics are quick growing and good branching. Those branches should be pliable, that do not split up at their joints. For uniform spacing among the blooms these qualities are essential.

Select a strong sucker with roots in February and plant it in 15 cm pots using the potting compost recommended for the final potting. The ramming of the compost is not necessary for this type of growing mums. It is obvious that the tips of the shoots must be pinched repeatedly to secure a massive head which should be dome-shaped. On the contrary if grown flat-headed the blooms will be more congested which is not suitable for a good display. As it needs a longer growth period the flower buds should come late. To effect this the day length or photo-period should be increased artificially. At night the pot is placed under a fluorescent lamp until the end of September.

It is obvious that a larger pot is required for the final potting. Generally 30-35 cm pots are used. Only one shift proves to be enough. First potting in a 15 cm pot and then shifting to the 30 cm pot after 60 days. Top dressing or liquid manure should be applied to maintain continuous growth.

In the Japanese shows a *Sen Rin Tsukuri* 2.25 metre in diameter and 2 metre in height with 200-500 blooms is an inconceivable sight. The blooms are not spray type. The training should be such as to producing one bloom per shoot. As the flowers are raised from the terminal buds disbudding becomes essential.

The staking for keeping the shoots in position and the uniform spacing of blooms is of vital importance. Insert 4 bamboo splits, 2 cm in diameter, at 4 equidistant points in the pot soil near the periphery. Including the central stake 5 stakes in all form the framework to support the structure that props the network of the branching system. The central shoot should be tied to the central stake. For supporting other shoots a dome-like structure with a number of concentric rings of thin wire-like bamboo strips should be constructed as shown in Fig. 22. Instead of bamboo strips galvanized wire (10 gauge) can be used.

Fig. 22: The structure of staking for 'Sen Rin Tsukuri'

On the 2nd February of this year (2001) I was surprised to see a *Sen Rin Tsukuri* exhibited by a young grower in the flower show of Siliguri (W. Bengal). It had 835 medium-sized blooms of the cultivar 'MOUNTAINEER'. The transport minister of the state generously awarded the successful grower a sum of rupees ten thousand. This year (2002) he (Mriganka Pal of Balurghat, Dinajpur, W.B.) has succeeded in growing a plant with 1130 blooms which was shown in Kshudiram Anushilan Kendra in Kolkata in January, 2002. Mr. Pal for his unprecedented achievement rides over his Japanese counterpart.

28
Growing Cascades

In Japan the large-flowered varieties as flat Korean, anemone and decoratives are grown in the cascade form resembling a waterfall. It is termed as *Kengai* in Japanese language. The plants instead of growing upright are trained to trail like hangings. In this process the main stem touches the rim of the pot and bends downwards. In the Japanese shows the cascades taller than 3 metre are displayed.

The tall varieties have to be selected for making cascades. The stem should be strong, that can be made pliable for shaping. A triangular piece of welded wire mesh of 1" squares can be used. The netting is tied to the stake. Stop the plant when 15 cm high. A good number of laterals will arise which should be pinched to develop more branches that will cover the triangular netting. Tie the branches and shoots to the wires of the netting with *sutli* (hessian thread). The growth instead of looking bushy will appear to be vertically flat. When the flower buds grow the central stake should be removed and the vertical netting will gradually be made to incline and finally its top will point to the ground at an angle of 40° to the pot which will be placed high preferably on a bench. A cascade chrysanthemum is highly suitable for room decoration. The cascades placed in the corners or against a wall look enchanting.

Fig. 23: Cascade

29
Pompons

The pompons can produce masses of blooms. Generally 4-8 hundred blooms are obtained from a plant forming a large bush. The largest i.e. a specimen pot should have a head of 90 cm in diameter.

The cuttings or suckers are planted in 15 cm pots in May-June. After 50 days they are shifted to 30 cm pots. The compost for both the pottings should be the same as for the final potting of the large-flowered mums.

Fig. 24: Pompon with a massive head

Stop the plant when 15 cm high. Then the tops of the laterals will be pinched to force more branches to sprout. The shoots will be pinched when they are 8-10 cm long. After stopping pinching for 3-4 times becomes necessary. To make the head flat apply B-9 or cycocel by spraying. Ultimately 200-300 shoots are obtained for bearing flower buds. Obviously the buds are terminal. Because no vegetative growth will then occur, only the flower buds will be appearing from the leaf joints.

Next comes the selection of buds. If comparatively large flowers opening at a time without being jumbled up have to be secured retain the central bud and disbud the laterals. On the contrary if more flowers have to be raised pinch the central bud and allow the lateral buds to bloom, as done in the case of spray-form flowering.

For pompons one stake at the centre is enough. But to maintain a neat outline of the head cotton thread is used to maintain the desired distance between the central stake and the leaning branch. First tie one end of the thread to the stake and the other to the related branch.

30
Care of Blooms

A chrysanthemum bud takes a long time to bloom. As soon as the buds begin to open care should be taken to protect them from the strong sun. When a bud begins to open the outer florets get tinted. Since then it takes about a period of four weeks to attain a full bloom condition. This period is divided into two halves. In the first half the plants will be placed under a translucent shed of fibreglass or polythene. The transparent fibreglass sheets gradually become translucent after their use in the shed. The transparent polythene used in making the shed in the early rains becomes translucent in November. Such a shed is apt to protect the blooms from both sun and shower. In the second half a shed of opaque but white polythene is useful. Because it provides plenty of diffused sun suitable for the growth of this stage.

Fig. 25: Bagging a bloom

In winter dry north wind blows. It is dry enough to desiccate the soft petals. So care should be taken to protect the blooms. To minimise the dryness at noon soak the floor with water which will raise the percentage of humidity of the surroundings.

The plants may need to be sprayed with the pesticides and fungicides. The blooms must be saved from these chemicals. While spraying cover the blooms with polybags. After spraying bags should be removed.

The flowers of the plants grown in the ground can be protected from sun and shower by bagging. Cover each bloom with a kraft-paper bag the mouth of which is tied to the flower stalk so that insect may not enter the bag to eat up the petals. Those who cannot afford to make a polyshed for few plants can easily use the kraft-paper bag to protect the blooms. The growers of a few plants are found to cover the blooms during the daytime and remove the paper bag in the evening. But in a cloudy night the bags should be retained to save the blooms from the shower.

31
Care of Stools

Chrysanthemum plants which have been exhausted after flowering are used for the purpose of propagation. Such stocks are called 'Stool'. Chrysanthemum stools survive till the next season. First of all, select the stools that produced first-class blooms. For the better management the soil of the stool should be changed.

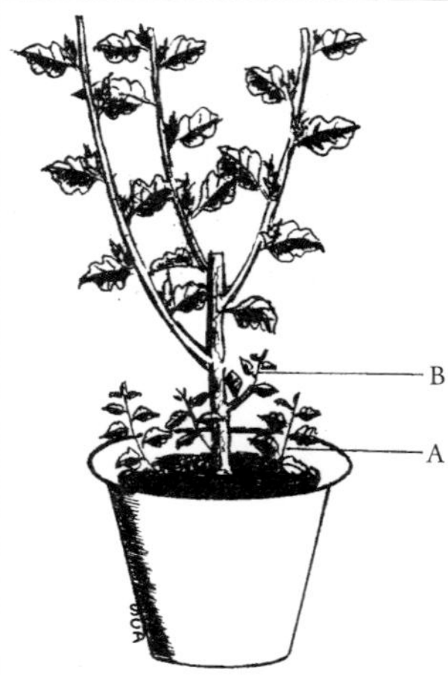

Fig. 26: Stool

A - Sucker B - Basal shoot

Prune the plants to half of their height. Reduce 75 per cent of the leaves by clipping. Then take out the plants from the pots, shake off the soils, remove the suckers and wash the roots with the running water of a tap. Spray the whole plant to drench thoroughly with a fungicide. After half an hour of this treatment pot them using fresh compost and sterilized pots. Keep the potted plants in shade for a week or so. The aftercare will be such as to make them a bushy plant that can supply plenty of shoots for cuttings.

32
Growing in Ground

Chrysanthemums are successfully grown in the ground. In the region where the rainfall is low, i.e. not more than 350 mm, chrysanthemum can be grown in the ground. The cut-flowers from the field can be shown profusely in the exhibition. Until the special class for cut-blooms is introduced in the shows as well as ground cultivation is taken up the entries in the shows will not be satisfactory.

In the low rainfall area the plants from the 9 cm pots are planted on the ridge. For this the ground should be prepared as per details given below:

1) In May the ground will be spaded and lime will be applied (100 g/m^2) by sprinkling. If there is no occasional shower irrigate the plot to mix the lime with the soil.

2) In June, i.e. after four weeks, mix humus and fertilizer mix to enrich the soil. The following ingredients should be mixed thoroughly and applied at the rate of 1-2 buckets (10 litre capacity) per square metre:

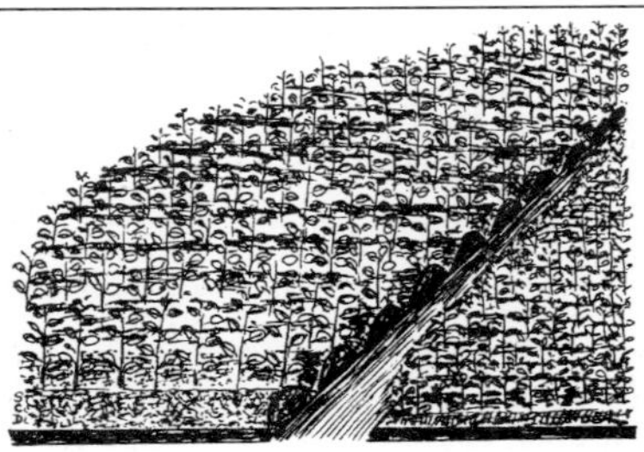

Fig. 27: Plants grown in ground are planted on the ridges

Humus (Leafmould /Farmyard manure)	10	buckets
Pulverized oilcake (Neem/mustard/groundnut)	1	kg
Hoof and hornmeal	2	kg
Bonemeal	1	kg
Muriate of potash	2	kg
Magnesium sulphate	500	g

If there is no rain irrigate the plot to decompose the manure mix.

3) Prepare the ground by spading and make ridges and furrows for the convenience of planting, irrigating and draining. The width of the ridges as well as furrows should be 20-25 cm. Obviously the ridges must run along the slope of the plot.

4) Plant the pot-grown cuttings or suckers 30 cm apart on the ridges. Stake each plant individually as usual.

5) Usually till the end of September no irrigation is required as there are likely to be frequent monsoon showers.

6) No supplementary feeding until the monsoon recedes. But foliar feed can be applied twice at an interval of four weeks.

7) As a preventive measure the routine work of spraying with pesticides and fungicides must be followed.

8) Generally the second crown buds are allowed to bloom, for which stop the plants twice as recommended for pot plants.

9) In the first week of October when the monsoon will be over apply top dressing in the furrows and irrigate. To hold irrigation water the furrows must have the cross ridges one metre apart. Liquid manure in lieu of top dressing can be applied with advantage.

The disbudding and desuckering etc. will be done as usual. After cutting the blooms of the crown buds the plants should be looked after as before. Because the flowers of the terminal buds which will be in plenty can be sent to the cut-flower market to fetch a lump sum of money.

In the eastern and southern regions of the country the rainfall is high. Still the few progressive growers in the district of Midnapore have been growing large-flowered incurved varieties such as 'Snowball', 'Sonar Bangla', 'Chandrama' etc. on a large scale for the cut-flower markets. With a view to getting a good price they are sending their mum-commodities to the cut-flower market of Mumbai since the middle of the last decade. They start growing since the beginning of the monsoon. So it is proved that the large-flowered and delicate varieties can be grown outdoors in the region of a heavy rainfall. The cultural technique is almost the same as given above.

The cultural technique especially for the heavy rainfall area is given below. And the same has already been published in 1987 in my book *'Chandramallikar Chas'* written in Bengali.

The whole area of cultivation should be divided in small plots of 529 sq ft (23' x 23') each. Each division should have convex appearance and a shallow ditch all around for drainage. This is to be done in May. A path of 3' width will run along the ridge of the plot. The beds will be laid out on either side at right angle to the path. The area of each bed should be 30 sq ft (10' x 3'). The adjacent beds have a path of 2' width in between.

In June apply 300 grams of lime per bed. After a few showers cover the plot with a mulching sheet of black polythene until the end of August. Remove the cover and apply the fertilizer mix (mentioned already) at the rate of six buckets per bed. After a few showers cover the plot again with the mulching sheet. After 4 weeks remove the cover and plant the cuttings from 9 cm pots 30 cm apart and stop by pinching the tips. They should be stopped again after a month for raising blooms of the second crown buds. The cultural operations like watering, hoeing, weeding and feeding should be done as usual. The plant protection measures to control pests and diseases should also be adopted.

Each plot (23' x 23') will accommodate 10 beds and 300 plants, i.e. 30 plants per bed. Thus each bed will yield 60 large blooms for exhibition. Of course in this case only two shoots after the first stopping are allowed to grow and the first crown bud is retained to bloom. Thus from a small plot of 529 sq ft 600 large blooms can be raised for exhibition purposes.

After cutting the blooms the plants should be looked after as before for growing countless blooms in succession for the cut-flower markets.

If the shows are held in the middle of January thousands of cut-flowers from the ground culture can be exhibited. The show authorities as well as the growers in the ground should consider the advantage of this technique.

Nowadays small-flowered varieties are being grown in the ground for the cut-flower market in the different parts of the country. The flowers of this type are in great demand in the market. The plants of the small-flowered varieties are very hardy, that can stand the frequent showers in the monsoon. So their planting can be started from the beginning of the rains even in the region of heavy rainfall. Prepare the ground and make ridges and furrows as described above. Plant the cuttings or suckers on the ridges at a distance of 45-60 cm. Stop the plants thrice and raise blooms from the terminal buds.

33
Chrysanthemum Sports

Most growers are confused with this horticultural term. So here it is clearly defined. If a variety shows any significant variation from the point characteristic to that type the grower should not be astonished. Because some varieties of chrysanthemum freely produce flowers quite different in colour from the rest of the plant. The 'Sweetheart' and 'Loveliness' families may be cited as the classical examples. It is sometimes experienced that the whole plant has become a sport bringing about a complete change in colour and form of the bloom.

Now a pertinent question, if any new strain can be obtained permanently from such sporting. With this end in view growers take the sported shoots for propagation. The plants grown from those shoots usually bear flowers with sported characters. If these characters remain constant for 2-3 years then you may expect that they have been fixed. Needless to say, the growers should desire to perpetuate those characters which are worth propagating.

Now I shall discuss the biological reasons behind this variation. The genetic term for such a variation is 'mutation'. The chromosomes of a cell bear a number of things called 'genes' which are responsible for the manifestation of characters. Because they are character bearers. Any change that occurs in them will be expressed in characters. If such a change occurs in the cells of an apical part of a plant the growth produced by that part will be of a new type.

To bring about mutations artificially radioactive rays like gamma ray, X-ray etc. are applied. Besides there are some chemicals which are also used for this purpose.

The sports are rarely found. But if a good number of blooms are raised per plant the probability of sporting increases. After flowering the plants are pruned to sprout more shoots, some of them may exhibit variation on flowering. If the plants are pruned in December the new shoots in their turn will flower in February-March. Much care should be taken to select the disease-free plants. Because if any plant is infected with the Aspermy virus the colour as well as the form of the bloom may be changed. At the early stage of infection it is very difficult to detect. In a heavily infested plant the leaves and even the stems are found to undergo a change. Sometimes it also happens that a delicate variety may sport a stronger shoot or a hardy variety may sport a weeker shoot, the other characters of which remaining the same. Thus in many cases improved cultivars are originated. On the contrary, some good variety may degenerate by partial mutation.

Apparently if a shoot seems to be a sport the flower should be plucked and the other branches and shoots be removed at the same time. Obviously the plant should be looked after properly with feeding, watering etc. The twigs sprouted from the sported shoot should be used as cuttings for propagation. The new plants must be observed with inquisitiveness.

34
Technique of Cross Breeding

The cultivars of chrysanthemum that are now grown in the garden have been originated from the two natural species—*Chrysanthemum indicum* and *Chrysanthemum morifolium.* The latter has a synonym which is *C. cinensis*. How the thousands of cultivars have been originated is described below.

In nature the new species or varieties evolve through mutation and hybridization. Before the development of the agricultural sciences nature since a very remote past has been introducing the plants of new characters. Nowadays the scientific efforts by the plant breeders have accelerated the process resulting in the numerous strains day by day.

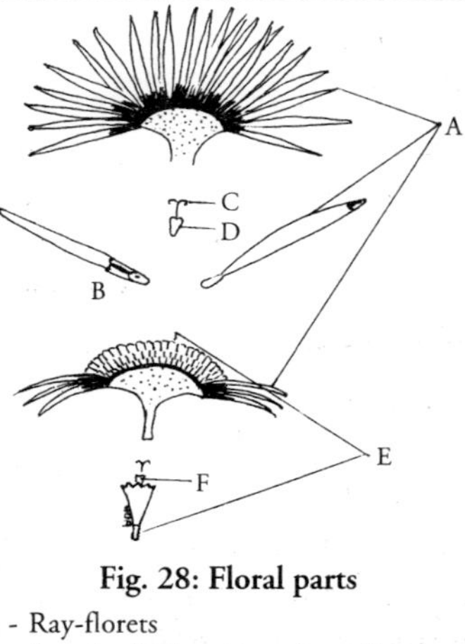

Fig. 28: Floral parts

A - Ray-florets
B - Longitudinal section of ray-florets
C - Stigma D - Ovary
E - Disc-florets F - Stamen

The process of mutation has already been discussed. Now the breeding technique is taken up. Fertilization takes place within the ovary of a flower prior to the formation of seed. Chrysanthemum belongs to the family *Compositae,* so what is generally known to us as flower is really an aggregation of a number of florets (small flowers) developed on a single flower head. The florets are of two kinds—those at the periphery with broad petals are called ray-florets and those at the centre are called disc-florets which are tubular in form (see Botanical Features).

A floret has its sex organs—the *pistil* and the *stamens*. The *stamens* are the male organs; when they attain maturity the pollen bags burst and the pollen grains spill out. The *pistil* is the female organ of a flower, the upper part of which is drawn out into the *style* which ends in *stigmas*.

The operation of the artificial pollination consists in transferring the ripe pollen from the *anther* of a selected flower by means of a fine brush to the *stigmas* of another selected flower.

It is natural that the more double the flower with numerous ray-florets the fewer and feebler are its *stamens* and weaker its *pistil* which is practically a great obstacle to artificial pollination.

The term 'double flower' is applied to the aggregation of florets developed on a single flower head having several concentric rows of ray-florets. Similarly the term 'perfectly double' is applied when almost all the florets of a head are modified into ray-florets. A 'single flower' means a flower head having a single row of ray-florets at the periphery.

The task of bringing about normalcy in sex organs is not at all difficult, which can be done by sustaining a plant in severe conditions and hardships. For this they are grown in less nutritive soil. A number of flower heads per plant are raised so that the available nourishment is divided among many blooms. Owing to the want of sufficient nutrition 'super-double' flowers become less double and a number of disc florets with their *stamens* grow and the *pistils* become normal, i.e. suitable for artificial pollination.

It is very important to note that the ray-florets are either female or sterile while the disc-florets are bisexual so they have both *stamens* and the *pistil*.

When attempting hybridization begin with the choice of parent pairs. Pull out all the disc-florets (leaving the ray-florets) of a head designed to be the seed bearer by means of forceps. Then trim the petals of the ray-florets with great care without impairing the sexual parts—ovary, style and stigmas. Collect pollen from anthers of the disc-florets of another strain already chosen as a pollen bearer with a fine sable or camel hair brush. Dust the stigmas with your collected pollen when they become receptive. A stigma becomes fit for pollination when it opens and emits a shining liquid which is sticky, best detected with a magnifying lens. The pollen should be applied very carefully, so as not to hurt the stigmas. Care should, however, be taken to guard against the insect or wind pollination before and after the hand pollination is made. So it is safe to envelop the head in a gauze. A dry weather is suitable for pollination. In case the operation is successful the ovule in the ovary will be fertilized resulting in the formation of a seed. In order to provide a dry atmosphere and moderate temperature the plant should be kept in a greenhouse the temperature of which should not fall below 60°F (15.6°C).

There are various methods of cross breeding. The breeders have their own fond methods. Many breeders also resort to pollinating with a mixture of pollen from several best strains.

Seeds obtained by a purposeful cross breeding should be kept in a separate packet recording the parent pair and the date of pollination on it.

Sow the seeds early in the next season and take care of the seedlings as usual. If hermetically preserved the viability of chrysanthemum seeds remains for two years. Observe the characters of the seedlings. If their ornamental quality merits propagation then take up their multiplication. In case you are not fully satisfied and want to improve it a question will arise, 'Is it possible?' The modern science will reply, 'yes'!

To achieve this select a variety that has some of the wanted qualities and take it as the pollen bearer, or father, while the hybrids of the first crossing will be the seed bearer or mother. Rear the hybrids of the second crossing and it is hoped that at least a few seedlings will display your wanted qualities.

It may also happen that the hybrids have got some entirely new characters found neither in father nor mother or in any other strain seen by you. A clue to the fact is supplied by the modern genetics which states that hybrids may inherit a character not only of their parents but of more distant ancestors as well. It is quite possible that the new characters revealed in your hybrids might have been possessed by their forerunners.

It is very interesting that you may grow thousands of new varieties without sparing time and labour for artificial pollination. The technique consists in raising seed by subjecting the plants to hardships such as the scanty supply of food, water etc. Grow seedlings from the seeds thus obtained. The new plants will not resemble their mother plants in many respects. The reason behind it is not at all simple, rather a very complex one. If a strain is natural, that is, not raised by cross breeding it can breed true to the variety by self-pollination. As the chrysanthemums we grow in our gardens are the vegetatively propagated hybrids their characters cannot be perpetuated by sexual reproduction. That is why when you resort to the sexual reproduction of your chrysanthemums, i.e. propagating by seeds, the offspring are apt to reveal the characters of their ancestors. The principle of the laws of inheritance in plant kingdom is a very complex subject which lies in the jurisdiction of genetics—the science of breeding.

Cross breeding is a very painstaking work. But the breeders' mind will be filled with great joy when success will be achieved. Many gardeners practise it as a hobby.

Raising hybrids: The seeds will be sown in the usual way. Labels should always be used to denote their parent forms. Transplant your seedlings in a rich sandy loam, well fertilized in advance. In case of food shortage use supplementary fertilizers.

When transplanting curtail three-fourths of their main roots. Always remove the suckers until the blooming is over. It is true that the flowers obtained this time will not bring out all the merits you want. It will be your task to make them perfect by proper nourishment and care. Henceforward adopt the vegetative propagation. Grow plants from suckers or shoot cuttings and follow the other cultural methods as laid down in the previous chapters.

35
Exhibiting

In the shows of this country mainly pot plants of chrysanthemum are exhibited. The showing of cut-blooms has been introduced in a few shows. Of them the show of the Indian Chrysanthemum Society seems to be the pioneer. Unless it is introduced in a show the number of exhibits will remain limited. Because the transporting hazards do not encourage the participants from a long distance. But transporting cut-blooms is not so hazardous and expensive. With the increase in number of the exhibitors the show authority will gradually feel the need of showing cut-blooms of chrysanthemum. A good method of carrying cut-blooms has been devised by M/s H. Woolman Ltd. of England, which is given here separately. Its popularity lies in that it is found convenient for availing public transport services.

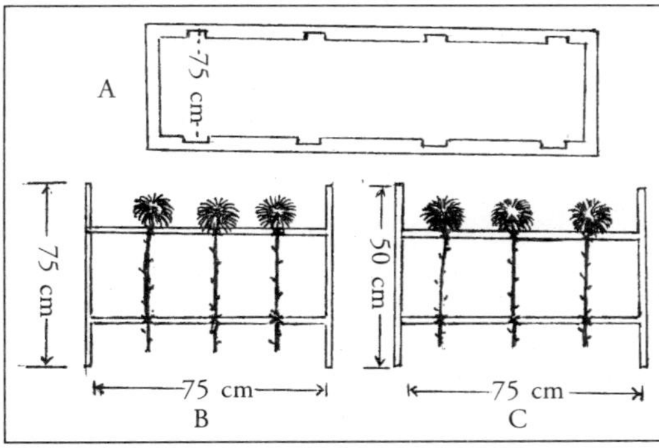

Fig. 29

A - Inside of a hurdle box with suitable grooves for fitting the hurdles into them

B - Tall hurdle

C - Short hurdle

The show schedule is published sufficient time ahead of the date fixed for the show. The plants will be grown accordingly i.e. the correct varieties to conform to the schedule. Secondly, the blooming must coincide with the show date for which the timing is necessary, which has been dealt with earlier. The following are the specimen show schedules that can give you an idea as to how the entries are made for exhibiting.

SPECIMEN SHOW SCHEDULE

(All India Chrysanthemum Show,
6th December, 1987, held in New Delhi)

CLASS VI (POT PLANTS)

Open to all exhibitors

The P.C. Paul Memorial Challenge Trophy for the highest aggregate marks in Class VI

Fee: Rs. 2 for each entry

Large-flowering cultivars in bush form

	Section	No. of Pots
1.	One incurved cultivar	1
2.	Three different incurved cultivars	3
3.	One bronze intermediate cultivar	1
4.	One white intermediate cultivar	1
5.	One yellow intermediate cultivar	1
6.	One green intermediate cultivar	1
7.	Three green different int. cultivars	3
8.	One any other colour, intermediate cultivar	1
9.	Three different intermediate cultivars	3
10.	Six different intermediate cultivars	6

CLASS VII (POT PLANTS)

Open to all exhibitors

The Sutton's Seed Challenge Trophy for the highest aggregate marks in Class VII

Fee: Rs. 2 for each entry

Small-flowering cultivars in bush form

Section	No. of Pots
1. One pompon (semi-pompon included) cultivar	1
2. One anemone cultivar	1
3. One single cultivar (Charms included)	1
4. One semi-double or double cultivar (Charms included)	1
5. One spoon cultivar	1
6. One spider (small-flowering cultivar)	1
7. One cascade	1
8. Four different pompon (semi-double included) cultivars	4
9. Four anemone, one or more cultivars	4
10. Four different single cultivars (Charms included)	4
11. Four different semi-double or double cultivars (Charms included)	4
12. Four spoon, one or more cultivars	4
13. Four cascade, one or more cultivars	4
14. Twelve different small-flowering cultivars, any type	12

The following is the schedule of the September show (1960) of National Chrysanthemum Society of England:

Cut-blooms of large-flowered varieties

The Johnson Challenge Cup

Class

7. Six vases of early-flowering chrysanthemums.
   Large-flowered distinct varieties, disbudded, 5 blooms of one variety in each vase.
8. Three vases of early-flowering chrysanthemums. Reflexed.
   Large-flowered distinct varieties, disbudded, 5 blooms of one variety in each vase.
9. Three vases of early-flowering chrysanthemums. Incurved and/or incurving.

10. One vase of early-flowering chrysanthemums. Reflexed, including white.
    Large-flowered, one variety only, disbudded, 5 blooms.
11. One vase of early-flowering chrysanthemums. Reflexed, white.
    Large-flowered, one variety only, disbudded, 5 blooms.
12. One vase of early-flowering chrysanthemums. Incurved, excluding white.
    Large-flowered, one variety only, disbudded, 5 blooms.
13. One vase of early-flowering chrysanthemums. Incurved, white.
    Large-flowered, one variety only, disbudded, 5 blooms.
14. One vase of early-flowering chrysanthemums. Incurving, excluding white.
    Large-flowered, one variety only, disbudded, 5 blooms.
15. One vase of early-flowering chrysanthemums. Incurving, white.
    Large-flowered, one variety only, disbudded, 5 blooms.
16. One vase of early-flowering chrysanthemums. Bronze or light bronze.
    Large-flowered, one variety only, disbudded, 5 blooms.
17. One vase of early-flowering chrysanthemums. Red.
    Large-flowered, one variety only, disbudded, 5 blooms.
18. One vase of early-flowering chrysanthemums. Yellow.
    Large-flowered, one variety only, disbudded, 5 blooms.
19. One vase of early-flowering chrysanthemums. Pink or Salmon.
    Large-flowered, one variety only, disbudded, 5 blooms.
20. One vase of early-flowering chrysanthemums. Purple or other colour.
    Large-flowered, one variety only, disbudded, 5 blooms.

The exhibits must be entered according to the schedule. If wrongly entered the judges will mark NAS, i.e. 'Not According to the Schedule'. Therefore care should be taken to make a correct entry for judging. The new exhibitors should take help of the stewards who make entries in the document and give instructions if sought for.

The exhibits must be displayed properly. Of the two exhibits of the same merits one showing better display will win. The display is also counted as a merit of the exhibit for which some points are allotted. Generally the pot plants are placed in the open, often in a sunny lawn. There while making a group of the plants of a section of the schedule the arrangement should be well displayed with symmetry, so that the beauty and glamour of the blooms are exposed to attract the judges.

The pot flowers should have a good foliage. The diseased and unhealthy leaves mar the glory of the blooms. For example, a woodpecker is beautiful with its crest just like a peacock. But if the feather covering the rest of the body is scanty or disarranged the bird will not look so beautiful. Similarly the flower and foliage together make a chrysanthemum beautiful. So for a good specimen the flowers and foliage must be good and unblemished. For this reason points are allotted for the different merits, including that of foliage.

The cut-blooms have enough scope for staging and displaying.

Cutting blooms: The blooms should be cut after evening or in the morning. The stem should be of the length of 30 cm or more. There is a question, whether the foliage should be retained or removed. If the stems are stripped of foliage the ornamental green foliage of other plants, that do not droop early, can be used while staging. After cutting put the stems in vases filled with water. After two hours the blooms can be packed for transportation to the show ground.

Packing: The cut-blooms can be packed in the cartons (paperboard box). The blooms must rest on a soft bed of loose cotton. The adjacent layers of blooms must be intervened with the spongy layer of cotton. Another process of packing is done by using a hurdle box. The blooms are vertically tied to the hurdles of two different heights, width being the same to fit into the grooves of the wooden boxes as shown in Fig. 29.

Staging: The large-flowered chrysanthemums, unlike roses, are put one bloom in each vase. Instead of flower vases cold-drink bottles are used extensively. Generally the cut-bloom sections consist of 3, 4, 5 or 6 blooms. The vas arrangement of them will be like this:

3 blooms	Formation: triangular, inclined or flat (in case of an inclined arrangement one or two in higher elevation in the rear).
4 blooms	Formation: square (flat or inclined at 45 degrees).
5 blooms	Formation: triangular or circular (the triangular formation may be flat or inclined; the circular formation is flat in which the central bloom is surrounded by the other blooms).
6 blooms	Formation: triangular or circular. The former may be flat or inclined with 3 blooms in the rear, 2 in the middle and one at the front. The circular formation is flat in which central bloom is surrounded by the other blooms.

36

General Rules for Judging the Quality of Blooms

The readers should always bear in mind that the main object of a chrysanthemum show is to encourage growing chrysanthemums of the highest possible quality. The judges and officials of the chrysanthemum societies should never forget that the responsibility with which they are entrusted is more than ordinary. They can achieve wonder by introducing a good show schedule for the type of flowers, number of blooms etc. and judging the exhibits with an unbiased view, i.e. without imposing any personal liking for any particular class or merit.

2. The exhibitors must have the liberty to stage their blooms in the show ground/hall abiding by the rules and regulations laid down in the schedule. There should be a show supervisor appointed by the authority, who will check the exhibits before judging commences to ensure that the exhibits have been properly classed. He should point out the accidental errors, if any, to the exhibitor concerned.
3. It is imperative to name the varieties. The error in naming however should not disqualify an exhibit, unless categorically mentioned in the schedule.
4. The judges should come to the hall only to discharge their duty to judge the merits of the exhibits in time scheduled for

the purpose. They should not notice the staging done by the respective growers.

5. Judging should begin punctually at the scheduled time. All exhibitors excepting the duly authorized persons and the officials of the society should leave the hall before judging commences. The judging should be done very quietly. The persons present there should not make any attempt to attract or distract the attention of the judges to or away from an object.
6. The judging should be on what a flower is at the time of inspection. What it was a few days earlier or what it would be in future is not a thing to be considered by the judges.
7. In judging a bloom the judges should strictly stick to the wordings of the schedule. Any deviation from it, i.e. to rectify the error of an exhibitor to enable him to win a prize, is evidently a departure from the act of judging.
8. If an exhibit of outstanding merit not scheduled for competition be exhibited, the judges, if satisfied, may recommend for granting an extra prize.
9. The decision of the judges as regards the relative merit of the exhibits should be final.
10. To consider a matter whether a person is eligible to compete as an amateur does not fall within the jurisdiction of a judge. The official of the society should always decide the matter.
11. Any protest regarding the interpretation of the wording of the schedule or the status of exhibitors should be accepted by the secretary within a limited time.

RULES FOR JUDGING

1. a) The best type of chrysanthemum bloom is one which has size and form, colour and freshness.
   b) 'Size' means a full-sized specimen showing the maximum potential of the variety.
   c) 'Form' means the approved shape of a bloom as usual with the particular type.
   d) 'Colour' means good colour characteristic of the variety.

e) 'Freshness' means the stage of its possible beauty.

2. *Foliage:* The clean and healthy foliage should be taken into account along with the other merits of a bloom.
3. *Staging:* It should be taken into account in all cases.

EXHIBITION INCURVED

Standard of Quality: An exhibition incurved bloom should have the shape of a globe as nearly as possible. The florets must be broad and nicely curved. The tips of florets should be rounded. The arrangement of the florets should be regular and close to form a neat compact mass as far as possible. Colour and freshness should be perfect showing no sign of staleness.

	Points
Form	35
Size	25
Freshness and compactness of florets	25
Colour	10
Foliage and staging	5
Total =	100

LARGE EXHIBITION (Formerly known as Japanese)

Standard of quality: A large exhibition bloom should have breadth and depth in equal proportion and be full to the centre. The florets should reflex gracefully. They should be brilliant in colour.

	Points
Size	35
Form	25
Freshness	25
Colour	10
Staging	5
Total =	100

Standard of quality: A large incurving exhibition bloom should have breadth and depth in equal proportion and be full to the centre. The florets must be incurved. Their arrangement may be either closely and regularly or loosely and irregularly, but in either case a bloom should have a spherical form. Florets should be brilliant in colour and fresh to the tips.

	Points
Size	35
Form	20
Freshness	30
Colour	10
Staging	5
Total =	100

SPECIMEN PLANTS IN POTS

Standard of Quality: A specimen plant should have a large number of high quality blooms and an abundance of clean, healthy foliage from base to top of the stem. There should be at least one inch of the main stem above the soil before it gives rise to branches. The branches should have a training to bend near the base and not near the blooms as to give a symmetrical form of the bush facing all round. Staking canes should not be obtrusive. The individual blooms should have a good display to the view. The height of the large flowering varieties should be at least two feet from the surface of the soil to the base of the bloom.

	Points
Number of quality blooms	20
Clean healthy foliage to the base of the branches	15
Good training and unobtrusiveness in staking	15
Total =	50

37
Soil Sterilization

The harmful soil fungus causes disease of chrysanthemums. The soil and organic manure should be sterilized before use. The potting compost after preparation can also be made fungus-free. The pots and sand for rooting medium should also be sterilized. The new pots purchased from the market can be used without sterilization. Similarly the sand collected from its natural source need not be sterilized. The old pot, old potting compost and used sand must be sterilized before use.

Pot: The steam sterilization of pots is conventional. The simple process for limited number of pots is as follows: Clean the pots first and dip them in water to soak. Then put them in a large bowl, shut the lid and place it on fire. After half an hour remove the bowl from the fire and open the lid to cool down. The sterilization by chemicals is also easy. Dip the pots in a solution of formalin (40 ml/l) for a few minutes. Then take out the pots from the solution and keep them covered with a polythene sheet for two days. Then remove the cover and use them for potting.

Sand: If sand is not sterilized the cuttings will rot before rooting. Sand can be sterilized by applying steam or the solution of formalin. For steam sterilization use a large pressure cooker or autoclave. Drench the sand in water and put in the pressure cooker. Put it on the fire and heat it until the steam is given out thrice.

For chemical sterilization soak the sand in a solution of formalin and cover the treated sand with a polythene sheet for two days. Then remove the cover and allow it to dry out. Use the sand when the formalin gas escapes fully.

By heat treatment sand can be sterilized. The process is called 'parching'. Put a pan on fire, put dry sand in the pan and roast it for some time.

Soil: Virgin soil should always be used in making the potting compost or it should be sterilized before use.

The soil can be effectively and thoroughly sterilized by applying heat through a process which is a bit cumbersome. The use of the chemical sterilants has become popular, because most of them can be conveniently used without the help of any expensive equipments. Chemical sterilization, however, is not as thorough as the heat treatment which if done properly eliminates all pests and disease causing organisms and weed seeds.

Sterilization by heat: For a few diseases in particular, heat treatment is still the only method of control. The best method of applying heat on soil is steaming. The steam of high pressure generated in a boiler is received in the sterilizing plant or apparatus. However this process is suitable for the big commercial growers. Large pressure cookers may be suitable for heating a small quantity of soil. A prototype steam sterilizer, which is not bigger than a big water bucket and used by the gardeners in the foreign countries, can be made as illustrated. This sterilizer consists of a galvanized water tank fitted with a metal soil container. The water tank is heated electrically from below. For quicker heating with least steam a nearly dry soil should be used. Because the moist soil would require much more steam for raising its temperature to the sterilization point which is normally 150°F (66°C).

Fig. 30: Bucket sterilizer

STERILIZING GARDEN SOIL

To grow chrysanthemums in the garden soil during the monsoon sterilization is essential. If done so the soil fungi and insects cannot do harm. By the following processes the garden soil can be sterilized.

Chloropicrin

It is also known as 'Nitrochloroform' or 'Teargas'. It is a colourless noncombustible poisonous liquid. By treating the soil with this sterilant, fungi and nematodes including all sorts of pests and weed seeds can be destroyed. Chloropicrin is very harmful to both plants and animals including human beings. It is very irritating to the skin and eyes. The police force use it as teargas in riot control. So it should be used carefully. A special apparatus, called 'injector', is used to insert the chemical into the soil. The injector has to be adjusted so that only 2-3 ml of the liquid is injected at a time.

The potting compost can also be treated with chloropicrin. Use an iron drum with an airtight lid. Fill the drum with the loam to be treated. Apply 35 ml of the chemical for a cubic metre of soil, close the lid for 24 hours. Then the soil should be left for about 3 weeks before use.

Methyl Bromide

It is, like chloropicrin, a volatile substance. Though not harmful to plants it is very poisonous to man. This chemical can easily penetrate the soil. It is sold in compressed gas cylinders. One kilo of the gas is required to treat 100 sq metre of ground space. After the application, the treated portion should be covered with a polythene sheet for 48 hours. The soil can be used for planting after a week of application of the sterilant.

Vapam ($C_2H_4NS_2Na, 2H_2O$)

Although very poisonous it can be used easily to treat the soil, 500 ml of Vapam (48%) is sprayed over the surface soil of 10 sq metre. To treat the potting compost, 500 ml of the chemical should be mixed with one cubic foot of the soil. Keep the treated soil in a moist condition for three weeks before use. It can destroy all sorts of elements harmful to plants, including weed seeds.

The gas is irritating to the eyes. No portion of the gas is left in the soil.

Mylon ($C_5H_{10}S_2N_2$)

It is as good as Vapam. Apply at the rate of 300 gm to one kg per 10 sq metre, depending on the formulation. Apply a drench or granules. The granules, however, should be raked into the soil. Cover the treated area with a plastic cover. Wait for at least 21 days before planting.

Soil Drench

Soil can be sterilized by applying fungicides like Dithane M-45, Bordeaux Mixture or Captafol in a liquid form. 0.05 per cent of liquid at the rate of 4 litre per 10 sq m should be applied. To control phycomycetes fungi of the soil copper fungicide like Blitox or Fytolan at the rate of 2.5 gm per litre can be used as a drench.

Granular Sterilant

Basamid Granular: An international soil sterilant for control of soil fungi, soil insects, nematodes and weeds and can be used for soil substrates sterilization (Producers—BASF India Ltd., P.O. Box 19108, Mumbai-400025).

38
Pest and Disease Control

Chrysanthemums are not easily attacked by insects as other garden plants excepting dahlia. If preventive measures are taken there is a little chance of being troubled by them. The weak plants generally harbour insects. The plants in a steadily growing condition are not found subject to pests easily.

PESTS

Nematode (Eelworm)

It belongs to the phylum *Nemathelminthes*. They are semi-transparent worm-like animals. There are two types of nematodes, e.g. free living and phytoparasitic. Their length ranges from 0.5 to 2.0 mm. The parasitic form climb up the plant and puncture the plant cell-wall by a protrusive spear. There is a kind of plant parasitic eelworm known as the 'Chrysanthemum Eelworm' that causes much more trouble to raise a good crop of chrysanthemum than anything else.

Chrysanthemum eelworms living in the soil move up on the surface of the plant through the film of water when it gets drenched in the rain, mist etc. The worms swimming through the film of water reach the leaf. Then enter through the stomatal pores of the underside of the leaf. Their free movement in the leaf tissue is obstacled by the leaf veins which act as the barriers. So they remain in a section fenced by veins. Getting the entrance into a leaf the eelworms start feeding the cell contents piercing the cells by means of a protrusive mouth spear which is repeatedly pushed into the cell, consequently the consumed portion loses its chlorophyll and turns brown showing a typical brown symptom of eelworm infestation.

Severely infested plants do not grow vigorously. Their growth becomes stunted. The internodes grow short and the plant gets a bushy appearance. As the infestation occurs from the base upwards the lower leaves show brown blotches which increase in dimension and ultimately the leaf-fall occurs. The older plants show symptoms more conspicuously. A brown discoloured region surrounded by a yellow portion and demarcated by veins is a good symptom of eelworm attack. The growers may think that only the discoloured portions of the leaves are infested and the rest are free from the worm. This notion may prompt them to take cuttings from a fresh shoot of an infested stool. They should bear in mind that their presence in plants may not always be detected by the symptoms especially in a dry weather which is unfavourable to show their activities. The eelworm may attack a flower bud also causing a partial or complete blindness of the bud. The absence of the normal healthy colour of a bloom characteristic of the type and the distortion of petals may be caused due to an eelworm attack.

Control: "Cleanliness will save from eelworm attacks." This should be the slogan of our campaign against the chrysanthemum eelworms.

The experiments have shown that the eelworm infested soil stored in a very clean place during winter loses its eelworm population completely. This is due to the reason that in winter eelworms cannot survive without taking shelter in plants. In winter the weeds harbour eelworms. The plant parasitic eelworms cannot have their food except from the plant body. Again, they cannot lay eggs when they remain unfed. Therefore, if the soil that will be used in the next season is stored in a clean quarter for a long time becomes free from the eelworms.

Before potting the pots should be cleaned thoroughly and sterilized by dipping them in hot water for five minutes. The potted plant should be kept in a place which has been kept clean for a long time.

To make the stools free from eelworms treat them with hot water. The bare-root stools should be immersed in warm water of 115°F (45°C) for five minutes only. Then pot them with fresh potting compost as usual.

If you apply granular insecticides like Furadon, Thimate etc. in the soil nematodes are destroyed. The roof-top growers can easily control eelworms by applying any of these insecticides at an interval of 15 days for a month or so. Apply 3 grams of the granules per pot for a single dose.

Aphids

One of the most common pests of chrysanthemum and the plants of the mustard family is aphids. They are gregarious in habits and as such assemble near the growing points. They suck the sap from the infested area thereby distorting it. Nicotine dust is an excellent remedy for this trouble. The dust or liquid prepared from dry tobacco leaves can be used to kill aphids. The insecticides like Malathion, Metacid etc. are very useful to control aphids.

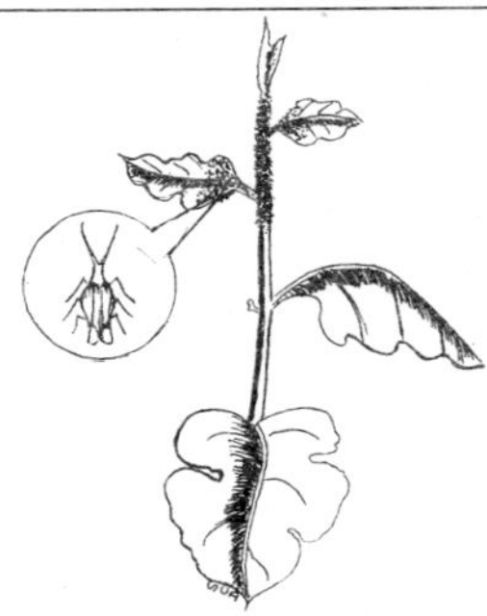

Fig. 31: Aphid infested shoot
An individual is magnified within a circle

Leafminer

It is a kind of pest that damages chrysanthemum leaves extremely. The small black female flies lay eggs on the leaves that hatch quickly into small larvae known as maggots. They destroy chlorophyll of the leaves. It is extremely difficult to remove the adult flies. However, the maggots can be eradicated by insecticides. Spray Malathion, Lindane or nicotine dust at air temperatures above 18°C.

Apply soot mixed with water to the soil. It will control the leafminer. Mr. John Woolman an outstanding chrysanthemum grower of England strongly recommends, "If watered into the soil it (soot) has the effect of giving benefit to the plant and also to a great extent renders the foliage more immune by the bittering of the sap."

Grasshoppers

A sort of green or brown grasshoppers eat up the chrysanthemum leaves voraciously. They can fly or hop to move quickly from plant to plant. They can be controlled by spraying insecticides at a regular interval. Many pesticides such as Metacid, Monocil, Malathion etc. are very effective to keep hoppers at bay.

Caterpillars

Caterpillars, like grasshoppers, eat up the leaves and leave excreta in globular form on the leaves. In the daytime they hide themselves under the leaves. In the evening they appear on the upper surface of the leaves. As their number is usually small that can be reduced to zero by a simple method of picking by pincers. The caterpillars can be destroyed by a range of insecticides especially those recommended against the grasshoppers.

Fig. 32
The grasshopper and caterpillar leave globular excreta on the leaves while eating voraciously

Thrips

A microscopic insect that attacks growing shoots and leaves. There are three species of the insect that infest chrysanthemums. Leaves become grey and the growth stunted. Spraying with Rogor or Sevin kills the thrips.

Mealy Bugs

The species that attacks chrysanthemums is *Phenacoccus gossypii.*

The size being 5-7 mm in length and 3-5 mm in width. The body of an insect is soft and covered with a sort of woolly substance. They are found to stick to a point as if they cannot move. The female bugs lay about 300 eggs at a time. The egg masses are also covered with a woolly substance. Ants help spread mealy bugs. They are attracted by a honey-like substance secreted by the bodies of the bugs. Mealy bug can be controlled by spraying Malathion or by picking with forceps.

Mites

These are minute insects (spider mites) that spin webs on the underside of the leaves, which can be seen well through a magnifying glass. The infestation of mites takes place in dry months. The affected leaves look dull because the insects are sucking their sap. Red spider mites, like mildew, are very obstinate and difficult to remove completely.

The mites cannot stand moisture. Spray cold water on the underside of the leaves in the evening. Any insecticide or fungicide based on sulphur can be sprayed to control mites. Kelthane, Lime-sulphur, Mit 505, sulphur dust are effective against mites.

Snails and Slugs

The snails cause harm to chrysanthemums in a very moist weather especially in autumn. They invade at night. A bait prepared with copper arsenate, lead arsenate or calcium arsenate can be given to kill snails. Metaldehyde can be applied in a powder or liquid form to destroy snails. *Mahua* oilcake in the powder form is sprinkled near the plants to destroy snails.

The slugs are like a caterpillar. Though soft-bodied they are closely related to snails, oysters and octopuses. Slugs hide themselves in the crevices during the day and come to the leaves or petals to eat them up after dusk. They move very slowly like snails and exude a slimy trail behind them as we see in case of the crawling snails.

To control slugs use the chemicals recommended against the invasion of snails.

DISEASES

Leaf Spot

The blotches or spots of brown colour appear on the lower leaves of a plant. Gradually however these spots turn black and become wider so that the leaves wither eventually.

The fungous attack causes leaf spots. There are two species (*Cercospora chrysantheme* and *Septoria lencanthemi*) which are responsible for this disease. The fungicides like Dithane M-45, Bavistin, Blitox should be sprayed alternately at an interval of a week. The infected leaves must be collected and destroyed by burning.

Mildew

It is a fungous disease. The species that causes the disease of chrysanthemum is *Erysiphe cichoracearum*. A grey powder-like substance is deposited on leaves. Hence the name 'Powdery Mildew'. In the moist weather the infection spreads.

To control mildew apply sulphur dust or spray with lime-sulphur. Any sulphur based fungicides such as Sulfotox, Sulfex can be used against mildew.

Stem Rot

The stem is rotted due to fungous attack. The fungus species which are responsible for the disease are *Fusarium* and *Pellicularia*. As a preventive measure use sterilized potting compost.

Wilt

A sort of fungus that becomes active in the rains especially during a downpour. The fungus causes damage to the growing rootlets. So the plant cannot absorb water, that results in wilting. This disease is not curable. But it can be prevented by using sterilized potting compost. Secondly, if the pots are not kept under the open sky, i.e. put under a polyshed, the plants are saved from the bad effect of downpouring.

VIRAL DISEASES

Chrysanthemums become victim of many viral diseases. Dr. Philip

Barly and his associates of America have done a good research work in this regard. There is no cure for virus troubles. The preventive measures are very effective. The insects that spread the infection should be destroyed by spraying suitable insecticides at a regular interval. Generally aphids spread the virus. So keep your chrysanthemums free from aphids.

Aspermy

It is a chrysanthemum virus. If attacked the petals become distorted. The colour of flowers is changed. The infected plant must be destroyed. It should be used for propagation. The change in colour and the shape of the petals may lead one to think that it has been sported. With the prospect of getting a mutant cultivar the grower may use the shoots for propagation. How dangerous this can be is imaginable. It is said that the eastern part of Asia is the source of this virus. Because the chrysanthemums imported to Europe and America from this region are found infected by this virus. If an infected plant is kept at 97°F in an incubator for 3-4 weeks it becomes free from this virus.

Petal Distorting Virus

The broad petals of an infected plant become narrow and incurved in shape. This virus is not spread by insects. It spreads through the use of cuttings for propagation.

Mosaic Virus

Dr. P. Barly and F.F. Smith of America have identified eight mosaic viruses that infect chrysanthemum. These spread through the aphids. When infected the green leaves get the blotches of yellow colour.

Rosette Virus

The growing point of an infected plant becomes thick forming a rosette of leaves. The internodes are virtually found absent. The growth is stopped, the flower bud does not appear. The plant looks very bushy with the emergence of a number of thick suckers.

This virus is not spread by insects. The infected plants should not be used for propagation.

39
Cultural Calendar

Chrysanthemum though treated as an annual is evidently perennial. So one has to do something through all the seasons of the year. As its propagation is easy one has to save the plants until the next propagation season is over. After taking shoots for cuttings the stools are destroyed.

January

The grower should start right from January to succeed in the next season. The plants that produced good flowers should be set apart and the others will be destroyed. These selected plants will serve two purposes. First, they will be reared as a source of good cuttings for propagation. Secondly, to enhance the probability of sporting the plants are pruned to force sprouting of many shoots. Their sucker growths must be checked. Because if the suckers are retained the stem would hardly produce any good shoot capable of giving flowers. Apply liquid manure in the middle of January. The plants from suckers can be grown if more mother plants are required, especially for those varieties which are then less in number. The plants grown from suckers in January become large enough to supply more cuttings in June-July. The old plants after flowering are pruned and reared as mother plants. The details have been given in 'Care of Stools'.

February

The shoots of the stools will bear flower buds. A few of them may open in the last week of this month. Then they will be checked with careful attention to find out if there is any sport (see 'Chrysanthemum Sports').

The suckers that were planted in 12 cm pots in January will now be shifted to 25 cm pots. The potting compost recommended for the second potting should be used for this purpose also.

The stakes of the stools should be changed. The new stakes should be used. Because the old stakes might give shelter to some harmful insects. Now a dose of liquid manure or top dressing can be applied to the pots of the stools if any deficiency symptoms are noticed. To prevent disease and pest spraying with a dose of fungicide and insecticide should be repeated alternately.

March

In the plains the temperature rises. So the plants will need more watering. The protection from the sun is not necessary. The plant protection measure, i.e. spraying with insecticides and fungicides, should be repeated even if there is no attack or incidence of pests and diseases. The sucker growths must be removed. The new blooms of the stools should be checked to see if there is any sport.

April

The temperature will rise more and the nor-wester shower may start. The chrysanthemums should preferably be placed in the transparent shed to protect them from showers. The shower-drenched leaves are very susceptible to diseases. Eelworms also climb up the stem and reach the leaves through the film of water. Soil, humus and lime should be mixed and kept in a heap in a moist condition for making potting compost in June. It is better if done earlier, i.e. in February-March.

May

The suckers or cuttings are potted by those who will produce hundreds of blooms per plant in December or January. For making cascades, *Sen Rin Tsukuri* and large-headed plants of pompons one should start right now.

Liquid manure should be applied in the pots of the stools. Now their heads have become heavy with branches which will be supplying cuttings from the next month. Additional staking may be required to keep the branches in position. Removing suckers and spraying with pesticides and fungicides should be done in this month also. Sterilize the sand and store it in large polybags, which will be used as a rooting medium in June and July.

June

In the eastern region of the country the monsoon starts in the middle of this month. Now it is imperative to place the pots under a polyshed. But in no way the plants should be placed in shade. The direct sunshine for the most period of the day is useful. The leaves affected by fungous and eelworm attacks should be destroyed by burning. The cuttings should be taken for rooting. On rooting they will be shifted to thumb pots.

July

From the thumb pots the cuttings should be transferred to 9 cm pots, which is termed as 'first potting'. The plant will be stopped by the end of this month for raising blooms from the crown buds.

August

The plants will be protected from the rains. The second potting has to be done by the end of this month. The plant protection measures should be adopted as usual.

September

Though showers become less frequent and the intensity is reduced still the plants be kept in the polyshed. This is the month of the final potting and for the third pinching for raising blooms from the terminal buds.

Those who aim at late flowering should do first potting in this month. And those who have no polyshed would like to grow mums when the monsoon will recede. They should now take cuttings for rooting.

October

The monsoon recedes from the mainland of the country in the second week of this month. Those who have no polyshed can perform the first potting right now. Instead of second potting they should do the final potting by the end of this month or in the first week of the next month. The plants grown early need disbudding to select the buds to flower. The top dressing or liquid manure is usually needed to nourish the buds. The routine work of the plant protection measure should be followed. For the commercial purpose of cut-flowers the cuttings from the 9 cm pots are transplanted in the ground.

November

The buds are now in the blooming stage. If the plants are not under the translucent shed the individual blooms should be covered with a kraft-paper bag. Now aphids may infest the plant. To check it Metacid-50 or Nicotine dust should be applied by spraying or dusting. A dose of top dressing or liquid manure is likely to be needed. The practice of disbudding and suppressing suckers must be followed as before.

December

This is the month of the flower shows. All the early shows are held in the fourth week of this month. Those buds which have opened partially, i.e. yet to bloom completely, should be forced to bloom up to the standard by heating. At the night keep the pot in a room, shut the doors and windows and put a bulb of 500 watt 30 cm above the bloom.

Appendices

A
FORMULATIONS/PREPARATIONS

Bloodmeal

Collect clotted blood from the slaughter-house and boil with water for 3-6 hours. Drain out the water and dry the boiled blood thoroughly in sun or in a drier. Pulverise it before use. Bloodmeal is used to supplement nitrogen for chrysanthemum. It contains 13 per cent of nitrogen. Analysis: N–P–K 13:2:0.

Fishmeal

It is a good organic manure for nitrogen and phosphorus. It can be prepared in the following ways:

a) Collect dry fish and pulverise it before use. It can be used as it is, i.e. without getting it decomposed.

   Analysis: N–P–K 6:5:0 + Calcium 5.

b) Dig a hole in the ground and bury the fish, fresh or dried, for several weeks. The soil should be kept moist during the period, especially when dry fish is processed. Then dig out the manure and pulverise it before use.

   Analysis: N–P–K 6:5:0 + Calcium 5.

c) Mix the dried fish with an equal part of *neem* cake, and keep the mix in a moist condition for several weeks. They should be used in a pulverised condition.

   Analysis: N–P–K 6:5:0.

Lime-Sulphur

Sulphur (*Gandhak*) 140 g

Lime (CaO)	140 g
Water	10 lt

Pour 5 litres of water in a wooden vat and add 140 grams of lime to it. When the lime starts reacting add the sulphur in a finely powdered form to it. Stir the liquid with a stick to mix the sulphur intimately with lime. Before spraying strain the liquid through a fine sieve. Lime-sulphur is efficacious against powdery mildew and mites in chrysanthemums.

Sulphur Dust

Procure good quality sulphur (*Gandhak*) and get it powdered. Strain the powder through a fine sieve before dusting. Sulphur dust is very effective against mites in chrysanthemums.

Bordeaux Mixture

Since the ancient times Bordeaux mixture is used as a good fungicide against a number of harmful fungi that cause plant diseases. Copper sulphate and quicklime (CaO), one kg each, are mixed with 100 litres of water to prepare a mixture of 1% strength. Soak the lime in 50 litres of water in an earthen pot and get the copper sulphate (Blue vitriol) dissolved in 50 litres of water in a plastic vessel. Then pour the contents of the second pot into the first pot containing lime. Stir the liquid to form a mixture of sky-blue colour, suitable for immediate spraying. Care should be taken to see that the mixture does not contain excessive copper compound which is harmful to the foliage. To test the mixture dip the bright blade of a knife in the preparation. If the blade gets rusty add more lime to the mixture.

A Bordeaux mixture cannot be stored for subsequent uses. It must be used immediately after its preparation. Bordeaux mixture does not need any sticker because it sticks to the foliage for a long time.

For chrysanthemum Bordeaux mixture and Lime-sulphur should preferably be used from February to June. Because they leave a white stain on foliage, which looks unsightly and lasts for a month or so. The chrysanthemum stools should be sprayed with any of these mixtures just after pruning.

Nicotine Sulphate 3%

Nicotine sulphate 40%	25 g
Quicklime (CaO)	400 g

Mix the ingredients in a glass bottle. Close the stopper and shake the bottle well for thorough mixing. It is very effective against aphids.

Tobacco Dust

Procure very pungent tobacco leaves from the grocer's shop. Get them thoroughly dried and pulverise. Dust the powder on the shoots infested with aphids.

Tobacco Soap Emulsion

Laundry soap	30 g
Tobacco leaf (dry)	30 g
Water	1 lt

The ingredients will be boiled until the soap melts (detergent powder should not be used). Cool the emulsion and spray on the aphid-infested plants. It can be preserved in a bottle for a few weeks for subsequent uses.

B
SELECT VARIETIES

LARGE AND MEDIUM VARIETIES

Incurved

Ajina Purple (purple); Ardhangini (mauve); Autumn Delight (bronze); Bravo (red); Bronze Turner (bronze); Bubble (white); Chandrama (bright yellow); Cossak (red with lighter reverse); Casa Grande (white); Dream Castle (rosy pink); Garden State (yellow); Glamour (yellow); Golden Plunder (yellow); Gordon Wells (canary yellow); Harold Habgood (yellow); Jacqueline Woolman (orange yellow); Jet Snow (white); Mountaineer (yellow); Naskar's Pride (white); Pink Cloud (shell pink); Pink Giant (cerise pink); Red Jack (orange red); Seiko Giant (rosy pink); Shin Mei Getsu (yellow); Snowball (white); Sonar Bangla (butter yellow); S.S. Arnold (white); Sun Antinon (pink); Temptation (deep purple); Triumphant (yellow); Violet Queen (silvery); W. Saunders (yellow); William Turner (white).

Incurving

Alfred Simpson (crimson with bronze); Apart (straw yellow); Barbara Philips (deep yellow); Bronze Prince (crimson with bronze reverse); Cavalier (primrose yellow); Christine Woolman (pink); Cinderella (pink); Classic Beauty (pink); Coronation Buff (red with buff); Coronation Gold (golden); Crimson Pretty Polly (deep red); Eva Turner (silvery pink); Full Festival (golden yellow); Green Goddess (pale lemon with greenish centre); Maharaja of Sikkim (yellow); Phil Houghton (light reddish bronze); Pride of Biren Bose (white); Rita Shirley (pink); Rustic (chestnut bronze); Shirley Monarch (purplish red with bronze reverse); Universe (deep purple with silvery pink reverse); White Cloud (white).

Reflexed

Autumn Blaze (salmon red with bright gold reverse); Beatrice May (creamy white); Bharat Ratna (red); City Beauty (golden); Freda Wilson (crimson); General Pitain (white); Joy Hughes (carnation pink); Mrs. Douglas Foxbill (red); Mrs. Helmypot (orange yellow); Peter May (purple); Roger Thompson (dazzling yellow).

Reflexing

Dee (white); Coronation Pink (deep pink); Kasturba (white); Shirley Superb (pink).

Spider/Tubular

Achievement (coppery); Adventure (pink); Chandra's Choice (yellow); Filtration (pink); Innocence (white); Kasturba (white); Mahatma (mauve); Puspahar (pink); Rupasi Bangla (white); Valiant (white).

SMALL VARIETIES

Anemone

Gandhar's Beauty (yellow); Pink Cushion (pink); Flying Saucer (yellow dwarf).

Single

Apricot Cleone; Atco; Autumn Shirley; Flare Path; Peter Robinson; Preference; Woolman's Glory.

Pompon

Balraj Shahni; Nanako; Sujata; November Bronze; Panna; Purple Star; Sonali Tara; Golden Climax; White Baby.

Cascade

Yuvaraj; Yuvarani.

C

CULTIVARS SELECTED BY THE CHRYSANTHEMUM SOCIETY OF INDIA

INCURVED

Chandrama	:	Yellow. Flower medium.
Snowball	:	White.
Sonar Bangla	:	Light yellow. Sport of 'Snow Ball'.

INTERMEDIATE

Ajina Purple	:	Rosy purple inside more prominent (Purple mauve).
Alfred Simpson	:	Outside bronze is more prominent, Bronze.
Angle Belle	:	Persian Rose (Mauve).
Casa Grande	:	White. At times takes good incurved form.
Cavalier	:	A shade of yellow. An obstinate cultivar.
Cover girl	:	Inside deep mauve is more prominent.
Dr. S. Mukherjee	:	Pink (Mauve).
Dream Castle	:	Mauve.
Golden Plunder	:	Deep yellow.
Grape Bowl	:	Inside rosy purple is more prominent (Purple mauve).
J.S. Lloyd	:	Light yellow. Sport of 'William Turner'.

Jet Snow	:	White.
Kikubiyori	:	Deep yellow. At times takes good incurved form.
Lili Gallon	:	Outside silvery bronze is more prominent, Bronze.
Louisa Pockett	:	White. An obstinate cultivar. This is wrongly known here as 'Improved Lousia Pockett'.
Mark Woolman	:	Light yellow.
Mrs. L.C. Philips	:	Yellow.
Pink Giant	:	Pink mauve.
Pink Cloud	:	Light pink (Mauve).
Rajah	:	Outside pink bronze is more prominent, Bronze.
S.S. Arnold	:	White. Very dwarf, good for Disbud Mini-Mum.
Sancho	:	Outside bronze is more prominent, Bronze.
Shirley Perfection	:	Mauve pink (Mauve).
Super Giant	:	Light yellow.
Thio Kinga	:	Yellow. Very dwarf, good for Disbud Mini-Mum.
White Cloud	:	White. Sport of 'Pink Cloud'.
William Turner	:	White. 'J.S. Lloyd', 'Eva Turner', 'Sylvia Green' are sports of this cultivar.

REFLEXED

Alfred Wilson	:	Red. Medium flower. An obstinate cultivar.
Coronation Pink	:	Pink mauve.
Cossack	:	Red. An obstinate cultivar.
Crimson Pretty Polly	:	Red. Medium flower.
Edith Cavell	:	Orange and bronze yellow.
Fire Flash	:	Red.

Florence Shoesmith	:	Red. An obstinate cultivar.
Gambit	:	Light purple (Mauve).
General Petain	:	White.
Gloria Deo	:	Red is more prominent.
Golden Thought	:	Yellow.
Green Goddess	:	Light green. At times takes intermediate form.
Jessie Habgood	:	White.
Lady Frank Clarke	:	Yellow.
Leviathan	:	Chestnut crimson (Red). An obstinate cultivar.
Mrs. W.A. Reid	:	Crimson (Red).
Phil Houghton	:	Chestnut amber (Yellow).
President Vigour	:	Purple (Purple mauve).
R.C. Pinch	:	Rosy purple (Mauve).
Shirley Monarch	:	Red is more prominent.
Sir William Mepherson	:	Yellow.
Woolman's Century	:	Centre light green (Green).

SPIDER

Diamond Jubilee (yellow); Mahatma Gandhi (mauve); Filtration (lavender pink); Red Quill (Brownish red), Gold Spider (yellow); Tokio (white); Green Nightingale (green); Tokio Pink (pink); Innocence (white); Valiant (white).

D

CHRYSANTHEMUM NURSERIES

Horticultural Arena, Kadamkanan, Jhargram, Midnapur (W.B.), Pin-721507.

Mrityunjay Nursery, Egra, Midnapur (W.B.).

Suburban Horticultural Gardens, Kulin Para, Khardaha, 24 Parganas (N) (W.B.).

Horticultural Society of India, 1, Alipur Rd., Calcutta-27.

Komal Gandhar, P-1/157, Congress Rd., P.O. Kalyani, Dist. Nadia (W.B.), Pin-741235.

Chandra Nursery, P.O. Rhenock, Sikkim.

Sarkar Horticultural Farm, 71 Jelipara, Khardaha, 24 Parganas (N), Pin-743155 (W.B.).

Pushpanjali, Vill. & P.O. Jakpur, Midnapur (W.B.), Pin-721301.

Kalyani Nursery, Kumudnagar, P.O. Nasra, Ranaghat, Nadia (W.B.), Pin-741201.

Shikherpur Kamala Nursery, P.O. Bagu, 24 Parganas (W.B.), Pin-743510.

Bansal Farms, A-267, Defence Colony, New Delhi-110024.

Rajdhani Nursery, Karbala, Jor Bagh Rd., New Delhi, Pin-110003.

Golden Nursery, A-2, Vikaspuri Turning, Najafgarh Road, New Delhi, Pin-110015.

Banerjee Nursery, 7, Ram Sita Ghat St., Bhadrakali, Hooghly (W.B.), Pin-712232.

Govt. Sunder Nursery, Near Humayun's Tomb, Nizamuddin, New Delhi-110003.

National Botanical Research Institute, Rana Pratap Marg, Lucknow, U.P.

Mita Nursery, Nai Dunia Campus, Indore, M.P.

H. Woolman (Dorridge) Ltd., Grange Road, Dorridge, Solihull, U.K.

Cotswold Nurseries, Cotswold Road, Worthing, Sussex (the nursery grows over 3,00,000 Chrysanthemum plants).

Keith Luxford Ltd., Sawbridgegworth, Herts, U.K.

Grove Nurseries, Swanly, Kent, U.K.

John R. Bell, Horman, East Sussex.

J. & T. Johnson, Tibshelf, Darby.

Wells Ltd. The Nurseries, Merstham, Surrey, U.K.

Dennis Baldwin FNCS, 8, Longcroft Nurseries, Laycock, Keighley, U.K.